HOME PLATE
COOKING

HOME PLATE
COOKING

MARVIN WOODS
and Virginia Willis

RUTLEDGE HILL PRESS
A Division of Thomas Nelson Publishers
Since 1798

www.thomasnelson.com

Unaffiliated trademarks: Grand Marnier®—Societe Des Produits
Marnier-LaPostolle Corporation; Crock Pot®—Rival Company;
Whirlpool®, KitchenAid®, Insperience(™)—Whirlpool Properties, Inc.;
Old Bay®—Old Bay Company, Inc.

Photo Credits
Mark Hill: back cover and pages xiv, 16, 30, 49, 50, 72, 82, 114, 136, 150, 168, 180 & 192
Kyle Christy: front cover, author photo, and pages 41, 57 & 146
Nathan Bolster: page 7
Edward M. PioRoda: pages 26, 37, 68, 78, 94, 110, 124, 134, 174 & 202
Greg Miller: pages 47 & 189

Food stylist: Sara Levy
Assistant food stylists: Gena Berry, Rebecca Lang, and Michele Philips

Published by Rutledge Hill Press, a Division of Thomas Nelson, Inc.,
P.O. Box 141000, Nashville, Tennessee, 37214.

Library of Congress Cataloging-in-Publication Data

Woods, Marvin.
Home plate cooking : everyday Southern cuisine with a healthy twist / Marvin Woods & Virginia Willis.
p. cm.
Includes index.
ISBN 1-4016-0202-9 (hardcover)
1. Cookery, American—Southern style. I. Willis, Virginia, 1966– II. Title.
TX715.2.S68W656 2004
641.5975—dc22
2004016258

Printed in the United States of America

04 05 06 07 08—9 8 7 6 5 4 3 2 1

From the crew in the kitchen to the folks watching at home,
without your support, *Home Plate* would not be possible.

This book is dedicated to you.

From left to right (1st row): Judy Sellner, Thelma Spight-Paschal, Virginia Willis, Marvin Woods, Michael Thomas, Elizabeth Palmer, Dee "Samantha" Enzmann, Jessica Keeley Neal, Julie Roseman, Stephanie Stephens, Cynthia Wong, Dolores Brown; (2nd row): Bryan Hartness, Tom Williams, Ralph Prado, David Dyche, Lisa Osborne, Gena Berry, Stephanie Smithmyer, Carol Rich; (3rd row): Gary Shaw, Craig Waller, Monte Johnson, Ross Hansberger, Jose Sanchez, Paul Cornwall, Jamie Murff, John McCurry, Jeffrey Noe, Clifford Stroud, Donna Stazzone, Jerry Taylor; (4th row): Tony Newman, Bob Simmons, Al Eastman.

CONTENTS

ACKNOWLEDGMENTS

ABOVE ALL OTHER INFLUENCES, I thank God for the many blessings that have brought me to this point. None of what I've experienced would exist without God's presence in my life.

There are also many people whose support I continue to rely on. In order for any individual to get through or truly shine on center stage, there is usually a group of people that believes in and supports him or her every step of the journey; I am no different. Therefore, I would like to thank and acknowledge key players at Turner South and *Home Plate* whose work makes this all possible: David Rudolph, John Parry, Mike Thomas, Veronica Sheehan, Virginia Willis, Thelma Paschal, Jamie Murff, Tom Williams, Monty Johnson, Al Eastman, Cliff Stroud, Wally, Tony (Hottub) Rob, Jose, David, Irene Foran, Sarah Hamilton, Nyssa Greene, Craig McMahon, Kyle Christy, Mark Hill, Edward M. Pio Roda, Nathan Bolster, Greg Miller, and Bill Taft. To the wonderful kitchen crew who continues to excel and put it all together: Gena Berry, Judy Sellner, Claire Perez, Samantha Enzmann, Bryan Hartness, Jessica Keely Neal, Vanessa Parker, Carol Rich, Julie Roseman, Claire Sellner, Stephanie Smithmyer, Stephanie Stephens, and Cynthia Wong. I must also include a special thank you to Cheryl Galway, Russ Benblatt, Mark Kempf, and the rest of the crew at Whole Foods; it is a tremendous pleasure to work with all of you. Huge thanks to Jan Walters and Karen Kelsh and all the folks at the KitchenAid Insperience Studio. Big shout out to my cookin' cousin Quito Mckenna and the Viking folks, A. J. and Sally Doloris; thanks for your support.

I am honored and proud to be loved by my family and close friends who keep it real and continue to support me in many ways: my wife and children, Petra, Chris, and Madison and my extended family, Terry, Monica, Raul, Aunt Flo, Aunt Rose, Aunt Margie, Vi, Cyndi Long, Kenny Hart, Uncle Charlie, Bayrob, Melodi, Cabiria, Lafern, and Mark. To my super star staff at restaurant MWoods in Miami, thank you for your hard work and dedication to being the best.

Last but definitely not least, I must acknowledge where the teaching and true support started; big thanks to my mom and dad, to my sisters Leslie, Lyn, and Erika, and to my nephews Manny and Kyle. Thank you seems like it's not enough! I am truly blessed and so grateful to have this many people with me in my journey.

INTRODUCTION

IF YOU'RE OLD ENOUGH to buy this cookbook, you're old enough to appreciate how different the world is now compared to twenty years ago when I was growing up. A quick look around and I'm sure you'll agree that times have really changed. Fifteen years ago the notion of a television network devoting time to food simply did not exist. American pop culture did not include familiarity with the names of top-notch chefs like Emeril Lagasse or Wolfgang Puck. Ten years ago, beyond Betty Crocker and Julia Child, big name chefs were largely unknown. Even on cable television networks (when cable meant more than twenty channels but not yet one hundred), food-related commercials consisted of restaurants and an occasional cooking appliance being sold for $19.99 on late night TV. Back then, food was entertaining only in infomercials. Today, *Home Plate* broadcasts to millions of homes, making us one of the highly rated shows on Turner South! And it's not just me; there's *Emeril Live, Hot Off the Grill with Bobby Flay, Sara Moulton, Jamie Oliver, Iron Chef,* and the list goes on and on. Yes, in the new millennium most Americans have heard of these shows, and many more watch them religiously, discussing their likes and dislikes around the water cooler. People are more interested in food preparation than ever, and they see television as a great way to learn about it.

So, who is Marvin Woods? Some of you are already aware of my "up north" upbringing. You know the Howell Township—"small-rural-Jersey-town"—story about the parents raised in the South and about the many summers I spent there as a child. But you may not know that I've enjoyed everything about food since, and because of, those days, from the aromas swirling around in the North Carolina humid waft of August to the spice from the sauces that would make you sweat while you licked your fingertips. More please! There was plenty, and you could have as much as you wanted until you were "full as a tick" as my grandmother would say. The sound of forks clicking against plates was usually a background rhythm for "Remember that time . . ." stories that made us laugh. No, I'm not a born-and-bred southerner but I'm as close as a born northerner can get to being one. This cookbook reflects my appreciation for a rich southern heritage.

Home Plate has brought the best of all of my worlds together. It is an opportunity to do what I love: cook, teach, and laugh. As many of you know, our show highlights a range of southern cuisine from buttermilk biscuits and skillet cornbread to brunswick stew and upside-down pear cake. And because southern food culture is so malleable, our options are endless, and we never get bored. During each episode I have the pleasure of teaching our viewers a new term or technique to enhance what many of them innately know from experience in their own kitchen. On the show, I like to call this "droppin' knowledge." And believe me, nothing gives me more pleasure than hearing veteran southern cooks like my grandmother and mother use terms like "braised" or "crusting something in panko" because they've heard them on *Home Plate*. It thrills me to know that my mother has finally purchased a quality knife set so that she can more efficiently "box cut" the peppers for the beef stew she's perfected over the years.

And then there's the laughter. If you have seen the show, you know what I'm talking about, and if you haven't see it yet, let me just tell you we're cooking for everyone: the rookies and the super busy bodies. Our goal is to strip away the mystique and horror of being in the kitchen, so we make it fun and simple.

What's next for Turner South and *Home Plate*? Well, with help from viewers and readers like you, we'll continue to create, educate, and have fun with the food you care about. And now we provide that to you in this cookbook. While some of the recipes you'll find inside are from dishes you've seen prepared on the show, there are many new ones. I'm particularly excited about Onion and Sweet Pepper Strata (page 21) because of its layering of textures and flavors. And the fact that you can make it the night before is really helpful. The "droppin' knowledge" tips throughout *Home Plate Cooking* cover a broader base than I do on the show. This cookbook is also broader in southern recipes than my last writings on southern meals, *The New Low Country Cookbook*. Since the low country makes up just eighty square miles, we concentrated on specific food from that region. This time the menu has greater depth and adds a refreshing twist to recipes like pecan sandies and apple walnut crisp. But don't get nervous, all your favorites are still going to taste great—just the way you like them.

Food, information, and laughter are what we serve up daily on *Home Plate* and the combination is unbeatable. These pages are designed to do the same. Enjoy and Happy Burnin!

STARTERS
& NIBBLES

First impressions are everlasting. This is why your starter requires the same verve you would put into the main entrée. The first morsel served should make a defiant statement; it should shout out—Here I am!—and dance excitedly over your palate. If it doesn't, why should the diner go any further into a mediocre meal? Would you? Remember, you want to avoid being boring and unoriginal with this first course so revamp an old favorite, or put a little twist on it, or try something completely new. Whatever you decide to do, keep in mind, you never get a second chance to make a first impression.

Have fun blowing folks away with these palate dancers!

LIGHTENED OYSTERS ROCKEFELLER

Makes 2 dozen

Oysters Rockefeller is actually a southern dish. It was invented at Antoine's Restaurant in New Orleans in the late 1800s to make use of the plentiful local shellfish. It was named for John D. Rockefeller due to the extreme richness of the sauce—at the time the elder Rockefeller was the wealthiest man in the world.

The restaurant has never divulged the original recipe, but it is said to include an exotic mix of green herbs and watercress, and it is always flavored with either Pernod or anisette. We've lightened it up a bit by cutting down on the butter and eliminating the heavy cream, but you won't miss the flavor.

1	garlic clove	2	tablespoons Pernod or other anise-flavored liqueur
2	cups loosely packed fresh spinach	1	teaspoon hot sauce
1	bunch watercress, stems trimmed		Coarse salt and freshly ground black pepper
½	cup chopped scallions	1	pound (about) rock salt
¾	cup (1½ sticks) unsalted butter, room temperature	24	fresh oysters, shucked, shells reserved
½	cup panko (Japanese breadcrumbs) or dry breadcrumbs	½	cup freshly grated Parmigiano-Reggiano cheese

- Position a rack in the top third of the oven and preheat the broiler. Finely chop the garlic in the bowl of a food processor fitted with the blade attachment. Add the spinach, watercress, and green onions. Pulse until the mixture is finely chopped. Transfer the mixture to a medium bowl.

- Combine the butter, breadcrumbs, Pernod, and hot sauce in a processor. Process until well blended. Return the spinach mixture to the processor. Pulse just until the mixtures are blended. Taste and adjust for seasoning with salt and pepper.

- Sprinkle the rock salt over a large, rimmed baking sheet to a depth of ½ inch. Arrange the oysters in half-shells atop the rock salt. Top each oyster with about 1 tablespoon of the spinach mixture. Sprinkle with the freshly grated Parmigiano-Reggiano cheese. Broil until hot and golden brown on top, 5 to 7 minutes. Serve immediately.

SAUSAGE-PECAN BALLS

Makes about 3 dozen

These bite-size treats are between a biscuit and a cheese straw, two southern staples. These nibbles are great for parties, around the holidays, or even to have around the house during a busy weekend.

Simply leave off the pecans if there are any allergies to nuts. Use turkey sausage to reduce the amount of fat, and feel free to use as mild or hot a sausage as you like. If using the sausage in casings, simply remove the casing before frying the sausage.

6	ounces ground pork sausage or turkey sausage
6	tablespoons (¾ stick) unsalted butter, room temperature
¾	cup grated sharp Cheddar cheese, room temperature
¾	cup all-purpose flour
½	teaspoon salt
36	pecan halves

- In a medium, nonstick skillet, fry the sausage over medium-high heat until it is cooked through, 5 to 7 minutes. Remove to a plate lined with paper towels to drain and cool.

- In a medium bowl cream the butter and cheese together until smooth. Sift the flour and salt together over the cheese mixture and blend together with a wooden spoon or spatula to make a dough.

- Crumble the cooled sausage over the dough and mix it in with your hands. Cover with plastic wrap and refrigerate to chill until firm, about 30 minutes.

- Preheat the oven to 350°F. Pinch off small pieces of the dough and roll them into 1-inch balls. Place the balls about an inch apart on baking sheets. Top the balls with perfect pecan halves, pushing the pecan into the dough and flattening the balls.

- Transfer to the oven and bake until they begin to brown, 15 to 20 minutes. Remove to a rack to cool. Serve warm or at room temperature. Store in an airtight container in the refrigerator for up to one week.

MINI CORN GRIDDLE CAKES WITH LUMP CRABMEAT

Makes 2 dozen

Fresh corn makes these bite-size griddle cakes more than just pan-fried corn-bread. These cakes, topped with jumbo lump crab and herb sour cream, are simply living high on the hog.

Don't buy canned, pasteurized crabmeat. Go for the fresh stuff, even though it's a bit expensive. Grades of crabmeat depend on the part of the crab and the size of the pieces. Jumbo lump is the most expensive and is composed of the largest pieces of white body meat. Lump crab is an acceptable substitute; these medium-size pieces are from the back fin. Make sure to keep the crab very cold since it spoils easily, and carefully pick through the meat to remove any bits of shell.

3	large eggs, separated	3	tablespoons unsalted butter, more if needed
1¼	cups fresh corn kernels, about 3 ears	½	cup sour cream
¼	cup yellow cornmeal	¼	cup chopped fresh tarragon
3	tablespoons chopped fresh chives	1	pound jumbo lump crabmeat, picked through for cartilage and shells
	Coarse salt and freshly ground black pepper		

- Place the egg yolks in a blender with half the corn kernels and purée until smooth. Transfer the purée to a medium bowl. Add the remaining corn, corn-meal, and chives and stir until smooth. Season with salt and pepper.

- In a medium bowl using a handheld mixer, beat the egg whites until stiff peaks form.

- Using a large rubber spatula fold the egg whites into the egg yolk mixture with a downward stroke into the bowl, continuing across the bottom, up the side, and over the top of the mixture. Come up through the center every few strokes and rotate the bowl often as you fold. Fold just until there are no streaks remaining.

- Heat 1 tablespoon of the butter in a cast-iron skillet or on a griddle over medium heat. When the butter is hot, drop the batter by the tablespoon onto the skillet, leaving about an inch between the corn cakes. Cook until small bubbles form on the tops and the bottoms are golden brown, about 2 min-utes. Flip and cook an additional 2 minutes. Remove to a wire rack to cool. Repeat the process with the remaining butter and batter.

- Combine the sour cream and tarragon in a small bowl. Season to taste with salt and pepper. Top each corn cake with a spoonful of crabmeat and the tarragon sour cream. Serve immediately.

[SEE PHOTO ON PAGE XIV]

ROASTED RED PEPPER & EGGPLANT DIP WITH PITA WEDGES

Makes about 2 cups

The flavors are intense in this dip. Roasting the peppers and eggplant brings out their smoky, sweet taste. Don't peel the peppers under running water or you will wash away the flavor. After puréeing the mixture, the trick is to cook until the purée thickens and the flavors intensify. Also, chilling the dip overnight allows the flavors to mingle and marry.

This is a great dip to make ahead a day or so before a party or to make and keep in the refrigerator for the weekend.

1	eggplant, about 3 pounds
3	large red bell peppers
¼	cup olive oil, plus more for the vegetables
4	large garlic cloves, very finely chopped
	Juice of 1 large lemon
1	jalapeño chile, seeded and finely chopped
	Coarse salt and freshly ground black pepper
	Pita loaves, cut into wedges, as an accompaniment

- Preheat the oven to 400°F. Coat the eggplant and bell peppers lightly with oil and arrange on a baking sheet. Roast the vegetables, turning once or twice, until the eggplant is very soft and bell peppers are charred, 30 to 40 minutes. Transfer the peppers to a metal bowl and let steam, covered tightly with plastic wrap, until cool enough to handle.

- Peel and seed the bell peppers and pat dry between paper towels. Peel the eggplant and put its flesh in a food processor. Add the bell peppers, olive oil, garlic, lemon juice, jalapeño, and salt and pepper to taste and combine well.

- Transfer the mixture to a heavy saucepan and simmer, stirring frequently, until thickened and reduced to about 2 cups, 15 to 20 minutes. Remove to a bowl to cool. Cover with plastic wrap and chill, covered, at least one day and up to one week. Taste and adjust for seasoning with salt and pepper. Serve the dip with pita wedges.

Marvin during Turner South's My South on Tour in Birmingham grating the Cadillac of cheeses, Parmigiano-Reggiano.

SWEET POTATO RAVIOLI WITH SAGE-BUTTER SAUCE

Makes 4 to 6 servings

This recipe is a southern twist of an Italian classic pasta filled with pumpkin or winter squash. Using wonton wrappers instead of making pasta is a huge time-saver, and easy, too. The filled wontons can be made up to five days ahead. Freeze on a parchment-lined baking sheet and then transfer, once frozen solid, to a freezer-proof, sealable plastic bag. Do not thaw the wontons before cooking.

These ravioli are topped with pine nuts to finish. (If you want to keep it southern, you can substitute pecans for the pine nuts.) Pine nuts have a light, delicate flavor and are commonly used in Mediterranean cooking. Toasting the nuts will bring out the flavor. To toast the pine nuts, place them on a baking sheet and bake at 350°F for about ten minutes until the nuts are golden brown. Pine nuts should be stored in an airtight container for up to three months.

FOR THE RAVIOLI:

2   pounds sweet potatoes
2   tablespoons firmly packed light brown sugar
2   tablespoons unsalted butter, room temperature
     Coarse salt and freshly ground black pepper
1   (12-ounce) package wonton wrappers
1   large egg, beaten
     Vegetable oil for the baking sheet

SWEET POTATO RAVIOLI WITH SAGE-BUTTER SAUCE

(continued)

FOR THE SAGE-BUTTER SAUCE:

6	tablespoons (¾ stick) unsalted butter
8	large, fresh sage leaves, thinly sliced
½	teaspoon crushed red pepper flakes (or to taste)
⅓	cup pine nuts, toasted

- Preheat the oven to 400°F. Coat a baking sheet with oil. Cut the sweet potatoes in half lengthwise and place cut side down on the baking sheet. Roast until tender, about 35 minutes. Scoop the potato pulp out of the skins into a small bowl. Measure 1⅓ cups of the pulp into a medium bowl. (Reserve any remaining pulp for another use.) Add the sugar and butter and mash until smooth. Season with salt and pepper to taste.

- Line a second baking sheet with parchment paper. Place the wonton wrappers on a clean work surface. Using a pastry brush, brush the edges of the wonton wrappers with the beaten egg. Place ½ tablespoon sweet-potato filling in the center of each wrapper. Fold each wrapper diagonally over the filling, forming a triangle. Press to seal the edges. Transfer to the parchment-lined baking sheet. Let stand at room temperature while preparing the sauce.

- For the sage-butter sauce, heat the butter in a medium skillet over medium heat until fragrant and brown, about 3 minutes. Remove from the heat. Add the sage and red pepper. Set aside and keep warm.

- Bring a large pot of salted water to a boil. Add the ravioli and reduce the heat to a gentle boil. Cook until tender, about 3 minutes. Remove with a slotted spoon. Drain well. Add the ravioli to the skillet of sage-butter sauce and toss to coat. Transfer to plates, drizzle with sauce, and top with toasted pine nuts.

HERBED TOMATO CROSTINI

Makes about 16 pieces

Meaning "little toasts," crostini are thin slices of lightly toasted bread, served with a variety of toppings—generally mixtures moist enough to be easily spread and seep into the bread. They are a popular antipasto, or hors d'oeuvre, in Italy. But there are no boundaries on fresh herbs and vine-ripened tomatoes.

Serve this simple snack in the summer when tomatoes and herbs are at their best. When selecting tomatoes in the market, choose those that are plump and heavy, brightly colored, and avoid those with blemishes or those too soft.

1	baguette
2	cups seeded, chopped tomatoes
2	tablespoons chopped fresh basil
1	teaspoon chopped fresh mint
1	plus 1 tablespoon extra-virgin olive oil
	Coarse salt and freshly ground black pepper
1	garlic clove, halved

DROPPIN' KNOWLEDGE

When seasoning food and you don't want to use a lot of salt or any at all, you can use fresh squeezed lemon juice to bring out the flavor.

- Preheat the oven to 375°F. Slice the baguette into ½-inch slices and place on a baking sheet. Toast until golden brown, 6 to 8 minutes. Remove to a rack to cool.

- Meanwhile, in the bowl of a heavy-duty food processor fitted with the blade attachment, combine the tomatoes, basil, mint, and 1 tablespoon olive oil. Season with the salt and pepper to taste. Pulse until well combined.

- Rub the toasted bread with the garlic. Top with the tomato mixture. Drizzle with the remaining olive oil and serve immediately.

[SEE PHOTO ON PAGE XIV]

MOZZARELLA & ARUGULA BRUSCHETTA

Makes 8 servings

The word *bruschetta* comes from the Italian *bruscare*, meaning "to roast over coals." Often served as an appetizer or afternoon snack, bruschetta is made by rubbing slices of toasted bread with garlic and brushing the bread with olive oil. Although crostini are very similar, in general crostini are smaller than bruschetta.

Fresh mozzarella is increasingly available in better stores and markets. This cheese is moist, soft, and delicate. It's miles away from the hard pizza cheese. Mozzarella was originally made from water-buffalo milk, but now most fresh mozzarella comes from cow's milk, both in Italy and here in the United States. Fresh mozzarella is normally sold in a container of water. It's highly perishable, so refrigerate it in its liquid for no more than a few days.

1	baguette or Italian loaf
1	garlic clove, halved
1	plus 2 tablespoons extra-virgin olive oil
4	garlic cloves, mashed to a paste with ½ teaspoon salt
1	pound arugula or spinach, stems removed, leaves chopped
	Coarse salt and freshly ground black pepper
½	cup shredded fresh mozzarella cheese

- Preheat the broiler. Slice the bread crosswise into ½-inch-thick slices and place on a baking sheet. Toast about 4 inches from the heat until golden brown, about 1 minute. Remove to a rack to cool.

- Rub the toasts with garlic on one side and lightly brush the same side with about 1 tablespoon oil. Heat the remaining 2 tablespoons oil in a large, heavy-bottom sauté pan over medium-low heat. Add the garlic paste and cook, stirring constantly until fragrant, 45 to 60 seconds. Add the arugula and season to taste with the salt and pepper. Sauté over medium-high heat, stirring, until wilted and tender, about 3 minutes. Pour off any excess liquid and transfer to a large bowl. Stir in the mozzarella, taste, and adjust for seasoning with salt and pepper. Divide the greens among the toasted bread pieces and serve immediately.

CURRIED HOT WINGS

Makes 24 wings

Curry powder is a classic spice of India, generally composed of ground coriander, nutmeg, ginger, cumin, pepper, and chiles. Mild to fiery hot, curry blends are as numerous as cooks. Curry is actually quite common in southern cooking due to the seaports of Charleston and Savannah.

The yogurt dipping sauce cools the spicy bite of the curry powder. The chopped mango is a crisp and sweet addition to the sauce. To choose a mango in the market, look for firm fruit that gives slightly and has a fragrant, floral scent. Don't buy soft or bruised fruit. The seedpod is long and oval. If you rest the mango on the counter, the weight of the seedpod will tilt the mango so the pod rests horizontally. Simply use this as a guide and cut to either side of the pod.

24	chicken wings
1	teaspoon Madras or standard curry powder
½	teaspoon ground turmeric
¼	teaspoon cayenne (or to taste)
2	tablespoons soy sauce
2	tablespoons canola oil
2	plus 1 tablespoon minced scallions
2	to 3 hot green chiles, very finely chopped
2	garlic cloves, finely chopped
	Coarse salt and freshly ground black pepper
½	cup plain yogurt
¼	cup chopped mango
1	tablespoon chopped fresh cilantro
¼	teaspoon hot sauce (or to taste)
	Sprigs of cilantro for garnish

- In a large bowl combine the wings, curry powder, turmeric, cayenne, soy sauce, canola oil, 2 tablespoons scallions, chiles, garlic, and salt and pepper to taste. Toss to coat. Cover and refrigerate to marinate for at least 1 hour.

- Meanwhile combine the yogurt, mango, cilantro, the remaining 1 tablespoon scallions, and hot sauce. Season with salt and pepper.

- Preheat the oven to 350°F. Transfer the wings to a baking sheet. Bake until a deep golden brown, about 25 minutes. Serve immediately with the yogurt dipping sauce and garnish with the cilantro sprigs.

[SEE PHOTO ON PAGE XIV]

PEPPERED TUNA KEBABS
WITH WASABI MAYONNAISE

Makes 24 skewers

Sushi-grade fish, available at better specialty stores and fishmongers, must meet specific standards of freshness, fat content, and firmness. When eating uncooked or barely cooked seafood, keep seafood cold at all times as close to 32°F as possible. Also, get the seafood home as quickly as possible; do not leave it in a hot car. Finally, store fresh seafood in the coldest part of the refrigerator until needed.

Wasabi is the Japanese version of horseradish. It can be purchased in powdered form from most Asian markets and better grocery stores. Fresh wasabi root is very rare in the United States. Wasabi powder has a very hot, sharp flavor and is typically mixed into a paste and served with soy sauce at the table as a condiment for sushi. In this recipe, we transform it into a dipping sauce for our lightly grilled tuna.

2	tablespoons wasabi powder
1½	tablespoons cold water
½	cup mayonnaise
1	pound sushi-grade tuna, cut into 24 (¾-inch) cubes
3	tablespoons soy sauce
24	large slices pickled ginger
24	wooden skewers, soaked in water
1	teaspoon freshly ground black pepper
1	bunch watercress

- Using a small bowl whisk together the wasabi powder and water until smooth. Add the mayonnaise. Cover and refrigerate at least 30 minutes.

- Combine the tuna and soy sauce in a medium bowl, tossing to coat. Marinate the tuna 30 minutes at room temperature, stirring occasionally.

- Meanwhile, preheat the grill to high. Wrap one piece of pickled ginger around each cube of tuna. Place the ginger-wrapped tuna onto a skewer 2 inches from the tip. Season the tuna skewers with pepper. Place the skewers on the grill and cook until just seared, 2 to 3 minutes.

- Line a platter with the watercress. Place the bowl of wasabi mayonnaise on the platter. Arrange the tuna skewers on the platter and serve.

SPICY TOMATO BBQ SHRIMP

Makes about 24 skewers

When buying shrimp, look for firm shrimp with a mild, almost sweet scent. If there is any scent of ammonia, it's a sign the shrimp is no longer fresh. Jumbo, large, and medium are all arbitrary designations. Chefs purchase shrimp according to the count per pound: 41/50-count shrimp indicates that there are between 41 and 50 shrimp per pound. "U12-count" shrimp indicates that there are "under 12" shrimp per pound. In general, 11 to 15 per pound are jumbo and 16 to 20 per pound are extra large.

To butterfly shrimp, cut the shrimp with a sharp paring knife along the back; discard the veins, and open the shrimp butterfly-style. Make certain not to overcook them. Shrimp cook very fast and when overcooked are dry and tough.

	Vegetable oil for the grill
1½	pounds (about 2 dozen) large shrimp, shelled, leaving tails intact, butterflied, and deveined
24	wooden skewers, soaked in water
1	cup Spicy Tomato Barbecue Sauce (page 15)

- Prepare a medium-hot fire and oil the grill. Starting at the tail end of each shrimp, thread the shrimp on the skewers. Brush with the barbecue sauce and arrange the shrimp on a large platter. Just before grilling, brush the shrimp again with the sauce. Grill the shrimp on a rack set over hot coals until just pink, about 1 minute per side. Serve warm or at room temperature.

SPICY TOMATO BARBECUE SAUCE

Makes about 1 cup

1	small onion, quartered
¾	cup distilled white vinegar
½	cup ketchup
2	tablespoons apple juice
2	tablespoons firmly packed dark brown sugar
2	tablespoons vegetable oil
2	garlic cloves, chopped
1	tablespoon Dijon mustard
2	teaspoons ground celery seeds
1	tablespoon Worcestershire sauce
1	tablespoon hot sauce
½	teaspoon cayenne
½	teaspoon turmeric
	Coarse salt and freshly ground black pepper

- Place the onion, vinegar, ketchup, apple juice, brown sugar, oil, garlic, mustard, celery seeds, Worcestershire sauce, hot sauce, cayenne, turmeric, and salt and pepper to taste in a food processor fitted with a blade attachment. Process until smooth.

- Transfer the mixture to a nonreactive saucepan over medium-high heat. Bring to a boil and reduce the heat to medium low. Simmer, stirring, until thickened, about 20 minutes. Remove from the heat and cool. Store refrigerated in an airtight container. Sauce may be prepared up to one week ahead.

BREAKFAST
& BRUNCH

It's funny how these two meals are like brother and sister and can be both very similar and very different. It is said that breakfast is the most important meal of the day. But breakfast can actually be a grind and a high-pressure type of meal. The need for an extra bit of sleep leads to a quick hit on the snooze button. When you finally peel yourself from your comfy sheets and give into your hunger, only a few choices remain: a bowl of cereal, a piece of fruit, a doughnut, or coffee on the way.

Brunch on the other hand, is a much more laid-back meal. You have time for a Bloody Mary or a Mimosa or the fancy coffee that surpasses the coffee you'd normally make during the breakfast sprint or any other type of refreshing drink—yep, more choices, and more time to make your decision.

You might think this is an attempt to do away with breakfast altogether, but that's not the case. Both breakfast and brunch have their place, but breakfast reminds me of the everyday routine and brunch reminds me of the weekend. So, maybe this isn't really about breakfast or brunch but is actually an attempt to add one more day to the weekend! No matter which recipes you follow, you can be sure that they are usually celebrated and eaten before 4 P.M.

Enjoy!

CORNMEAL BUTTERMILK PANCAKES

Makes 10 pancakes

The cornmeal in these pancakes gives them a nice crunch and a decidedly southern flair. The two leaveners, baking soda and baking powder, combined with the buttermilk, give them quite a lift. They are fluffy and light. Don't make the batter too far ahead or it will rise too quickly and fall. It's best instead to organize all the ingredients and then assemble the batter at the last minute.

Try these pancakes with Turkey Sausage Patties (page 20) and Savory Sautéed Apples (page 28) for a warm and satisfying breakfast or brunch.

¾	cup unbleached all-purpose flour
¾	cup yellow cornmeal
2	tablespoons sugar
½	teaspoon baking powder
½	teaspoon baking soda
½	teaspoon salt
1¼	cups buttermilk
2	large eggs, lightly beaten
3	tablespoons unsalted butter, melted, cooled
	Vegetable oil for pan
	Unsalted butter, room temperature, for serving
	Maple syrup for serving

- Using a large bowl, sift together the flour, cornmeal, sugar, baking powder, baking soda, and salt. In a medium bowl whisk together the buttermilk, eggs, and melted butter. Add the buttermilk mixture to the dry ingredients and whisk until just combined.

- Preheat the oven to 200°F. Lightly coat a large, heavy-bottom sauté pan with vegetable oil. Heat over medium heat. Pour ½ cup batter for each pancake into the pan without crowding. Cook until bubbles on the tops burst and the bottoms are golden brown, 1 to 1½ minutes. Flip the pancakes and cook until golden, about 1 minute. Transfer to a baking sheet and place in the oven to keep warm. Repeat with the remaining batter, adding more oil to pan as necessary. Serve warm with butter and maple syrup.

TURKEY SAUSAGE PATTIES

Makes 8 patties

The addition of the grated pear in this recipe adds much-needed moisture and texture since turkey is so much lower in fat than pork. Try an apple for a slightly different change in taste. It's best to use a combination of ground light and dark turkey meat. Ground white meat alone is very low in fat and can be too dry. Ground dark meat balances things out.

This recipe can easily be doubled or tripled. If you are feeling ambitious, make a lot and freeze them individually for later use. To taste for seasoning before frying the whole lot, fry or even microwave a teaspoon or so. That way you can taste and adjust for seasoning before cooking.

¾	pound ground turkey
1	medium firm pear, peeled, cored, and coarsely grated
¼	cup chopped fresh flat-leaf parsley
1	tablespoon chopped fresh sage
1	tablespoon chopped fresh rosemary
¼	teaspoon ground allspice
1	large egg, lightly beaten
	Coarse salt and freshly ground black pepper
2	tablespoons vegetable oil

- Combine the turkey, pear, parsley, sage, rosemary, allspice, and egg in a large bowl. Season with salt and pepper.
- Line a tray with parchment paper. Using your hands moistened with water, form 8 patties about 3 inches in diameter. Place on parchment-lined tray and refrigerate until firm, about 30 minutes.
- Heat the vegetable oil in a large sauté pan over medium-high heat.
- Cook the patties until browned on each side and the juices run clear, about 3 minutes per side. Serve immediately.

DROPPIN' KNOWLEDGE

Because microwaves cook unevenly, certain precautions need to be taken when cooking and reheating foods:

· Cover food with a plastic wrap.

· If it is not a rotating microwave, turn the dish several times during cooking.

· Use a thermometer to check the temperature in different areas. The temperature should be 165°F in finished foods.

ONION & SWEET PEPPER STRATA

Makes 8 servings

Strata is the plural of *stratum*, and in some senses can be singular. It may sound pretty complicated, but it basically refers to layering. This breakfast casserole is layered and bound with custard, almost like a savory bread pudding.

The great thing about a strata is that you can make it (and indeed should make it) the night before. Then in the morning, all you have to do is set it out at room temperature to take the chill off and bake it. If you want to add a little heat and make it spicy, you can add cayenne or hot sauce to taste.

2	tablespoons olive oil, plus more for dish
1	medium Vidalia onion, thinly sliced
1	red bell pepper, seeded and thinly sliced
1	yellow bell pepper, seeded and thinly sliced
2	garlic cloves, finely chopped
12	thin slices firm white sandwich bread, cut into 1-inch squares
2	ounces freshly grated Parmigiano-Reggiano cheese, divided
6	large eggs, lightly beaten
2½	cups milk
2	sprigs thyme, leaves picked
	Coarse salt and freshly ground black pepper

- Oil a 13 x 9 x 2-inch baking dish. Using a large sauté pan over medium heat, add the oil and sauté the onion until golden, about 5 minutes. Add the bell peppers and sauté until tender, about 5 minutes. Add the garlic and sauté until fragrant, 45 to 60 seconds.

- Place half the bread squares in the baking dish and top with half the vegetables. Sprinkle half the Parmigiano-Reggiano cheese over the vegetables and top with the remaining bread and vegetables.

- Whisk together the eggs, milk, and thyme in a medium bowl. Season with salt and pepper. Pour over the bread and vegetables. Cover and refrigerate the strata at least 3 and up to 12 hours.

- Preheat the oven to 375°F. Let the strata stand at room temperature for 20 minutes. Sprinkle the remaining Parmigiano-Reggiano cheese over the strata and bake until puffed and golden brown around the edges, about 50 minutes. Remove to a rack to cool slightly. Serve immediately.

[SEE PHOTO ON PAGE 16]

FRENCH TOAST CASSEROLE

Makes 8 servings

Maple syrup is traditionally used on French toast, pancakes, and waffles or as an ice cream topping. Pure maple syrup is made by the evaporation of the sap from maple trees. Maple-blended syrup is a mixture of maple syrup and cane syrups, resulting in a milder, less expensive, and lower quality product.

This casserole, like the strata, benefits from being made the night before. The bread soaks up the custard, resulting in a smooth, creamy texture.

⅓	cup (5 tablespoons) unsalted butter, melted
2	tablespoons light corn syrup
¾	cup firmly packed light brown sugar
1	loaf French bread
8	large eggs, lightly beaten
1	cup milk
1	tablespoon pure vanilla extract
1	teaspoon ground ginger
½	teaspoon salt
½	cup chopped walnuts
	Confectioners' sugar for serving
	Maple syrup for serving

- Combine the butter, corn syrup, and brown sugar in a medium bowl. Pour into a 9 x 13-inch baking dish. With a serrated knife, cut the bread into 1-inch-thick slices and layer them over the mixture.

- In a second bowl whisk together the eggs, milk, vanilla, ginger, and salt. Pour over the bread, allowing the slices to absorb the egg mixture. Top with the walnuts, cover, and refrigerate for at least 3 hours and preferably overnight.

- Preheat the oven to 350°F. Let the casserole stand at room temperature 20 minutes. Bake until puffed and golden brown, about 45 minutes. Serve immediately with the confectioners' sugar and maple syrup.

BLUEBERRY CORNMEAL MUFFINS

Makes 10 muffins

Blueberries make you think of purple-blue stained fingers, fruity summer desserts, and fresh-from-the-oven muffins. When buying blueberries, look for plump, firm, fresh blueberries that are a light, powdery blue-gray color. If covered properly and refrigerated, fresh blueberries will keep up to three weeks.

When blueberries are in season and affordable, freeze them in a single layer on a rimmed sheet pan. Once they are frozen solid they can be transferred to a freezer-safe plastic bag. Out of season, to reduce color streaking when baking with blueberries, use hard-frozen blueberries that are not thawed.

1	cup self-rising cornmeal mix
1	cup self-rising flour
$\frac{1}{3}$	cup sugar
$\frac{1}{2}$	teaspoon salt
1	large egg, lightly beaten
1	cup milk
$\frac{1}{4}$	cup vegetable oil
$\frac{3}{4}$	cup fresh or frozen blueberries
	Unsalted butter, room temperature for serving

- Preheat the oven to 400°F. Coat ten muffin cups with cooking spray.
- In a medium mixing bowl combine the cornmeal mix, flour, sugar, and salt. Make a well in the center. Combine the egg, milk, and oil. Add to the dry ingredients, stirring until just moistened.
- Using a rubber spatula, gently fold in the blueberries. Fill the prepared muffin cups about two-thirds full. Bake until golden brown, 20 to 25 minutes.
- Run a knife around the outer edge of the muffins, invert onto a wire rack, and cool slightly. Serve warm immediately with room-temperature butter.

CRISPY CORNMEAL CAKES

Makes 6 servings

Southerners have always eaten a lot of corn—fresh corn in season, dried corn in the winter, and cornmeal all year around in the form of grits. Grits benefit from cooking with milk or cream. But grits have traditionally been food for the poor, and of course the poor would use water instead of milk.

These corn cakes are essentially fried grits. Grits are a version of cornmeal much like the Italian polenta. Most Italian recipes for polenta can be easily adapted for grits.

5	cups water
2	plus 2 tablespoons olive oil, plus more for the pan and frying
1	cup coarse-ground yellow cornmeal
4	scallions, very finely chopped
2	tablespoons finely chopped fresh herbs such as parsley, sage, and thyme
¼	cup freshly grated Parmigiano-Reggiano cheese
	Coarse salt and freshly ground black pepper

- Brush a rimmed baking sheet with oil. Bring the water and 2 tablespoons olive oil to a boil in a large saucepan over medium-high heat. Slowly whisk in the cornmeal, stirring constantly to prevent lumping. Return to a boil. Reduce the heat and simmer, stirring frequently, until the cornmeal is tender, about 30 minutes.

- While the cornmeal is cooking, heat the remaining 2 tablespoons olive oil in a large skillet over medium-high heat. Add the scallions and cook until soft, 5 to 6 minutes. Remove from the heat.

- Remove the cornmeal from the heat and add the scallions, herbs, cheese, and salt and pepper to taste. Pour into the prepared baking sheet and spread out to 1-inch thickness. Cover with plastic film pressed flush to the surface to prevent a skin from forming. Refrigerate until firm, about 1 hour.

- Cut the cornmeal into 2-inch squares. Heat oil in a large, nonstick skillet over medium heat. Add a single layer of the cornmeal cakes and cook until browned and crispy, about 5 minutes per side. Repeat with the remaining squares. Serve immediately.

FRIED GRITS

Makes 4 to 6 servings

This is a classic recipe for reusing and recycling leftover grits. In the restaurant business it's important not to throw anything away that's still good. Use these crispy, fried grits as a base for scrambled eggs, sautéed mushrooms, or even sautéed shrimp with tomatoes.

The slices are coated in a light layer of self-rising flour that contains flour, salt, and leavening agents. If a recipe such as this calls for self-rising flour and you have only all-purpose, here's how you can make your own. For each cup of all-purpose flour, add one and one-half teaspoons baking soda and one-half teaspoon salt and mix to combine. Self-rising flour gives these fried grits a crispy crust.

4	cups water
1	teaspoon salt
1	cup quick grits
	Freshly ground black pepper
	Self-rising flour for frying
	Canola or peanut oil for the loaf pan and for frying

- Grease an 8 x 4-inch loaf pan. Combine the water and salt in a large saucepan. Bring to a boil over high heat. Gradually stir in the grits and reduce the heat to simmer. Cover and cook, stirring occasionally, until creamy, 5 to 7 minutes. Taste and adjust for seasoning with salt and the pepper.

- Pour the cooked grits into the prepared loaf pan. Cool slightly. Cover tightly with plastic wrap and refrigerate until firm, at least 2 hours.

- Invert the grits loaf onto a clean work surface. Cut into ½-inch slices. Place the self-rising flour in a shallow bowl and season lightly with salt and pepper. Add the grits slices and turn to coat. Shake to remove the excess flour. Heat about ¼ inch oil over medium heat. Fry the grits slices a few at a time until golden brown on both sides, 3 to 5 minutes. Transfer to a plate lined with paper towels. Season to taste with salt and pepper. Serve immediately.

FRIED GREEN TOMATOES

Makes 6 servings

Fried green tomatoes are as deeply rooted in southern culture as a field of kudzu. You can use peanut oil for frying, but for an extra southern twist, use a mixture of peanut oil and bacon grease.

Don't make the mistake of coating too many tomatoes at a time. The coating won't stick and the tomatoes might get soggy. Set up a workstation with the eggs and dry ingredients leading to the skillet of oil. Your tomatoes will taste better and it will help with cleanup.

6	medium very green tomatoes with skin
2	large eggs, lightly beaten
	Coarse salt and freshly ground black pepper
$3/4$	cup fine-ground white cornmeal
$3/4$	cup all-purpose flour
1	cup peanut oil or a mixture of oil and bacon drippings

- Remove the stems of the tomatoes. Using a serrated knife, slice crosswise into slices about $1/4$ inch thick. Season the eggs with salt and pepper. Combine the cornmeal and flour in a second shallow bowl and season with salt and pepper.

- Season the sliced tomatoes a few at a time with salt and pepper.

- Heat the oil in a skillet over medium heat. When it is hot but not smoking, dip the slices of tomato one at a time in the beaten eggs, letting the excess drain back into the bowl. Roll the tomatoes quickly in the breading, gently shake off the excess, and slip them into the hot skillet. Fry the tomato slices until they are golden on the bottom, about 3 minutes, and then gently turn them with a spatula and continue cooking until both sides are golden. Drain them briefly on a plate lined with paper towels. Season to taste with salt and pepper and serve immediately.

SAVORY SAUTÉED APPLES

Makes 6 to 8 servings

These savory apples are equally at home for breakfast with oatmeal or as a side dish for roast pork or turkey. The key is not to overdo it with the sugar or the spices and let the natural sweetness of the apples be the star.

Rub cut apples with lemon juice to prevent them from turning brown or store them in a bowl of cold water with lemon. This recipe can easily be doubled or tripled for a crowd.

3	tablespoons unsalted butter
1	sprig fresh thyme
4	large Granny Smith apples, peeled, cored, and sliced
1	tablespoon sugar (or to taste)
1	teaspoon ground cinnamon
1	teaspoon ground ginger
1	tablespoon fresh lemon juice
	Coarse salt and freshly ground black pepper

• Melt the butter in a large, heavy-bottom sauté pan over medium-high heat. Add the thyme and apples and cook, stirring occasionally, for 5 minutes or until softened. Sprinkle with the sugar, cinnamon, and ginger, and cook over medium heat, stirring occasionally, until tender, 5 to 10 minutes. Add the lemon juice and stir to combine. Taste and adjust for seasoning with the salt and pepper. Serve immediately.

HONEY GRILLED PINEAPPLE

Makes 6 servings

When it comes to choosing the perfect pineapple, it's all about the scent. If it smells ripe and fruity, it is. Choose plump, heavy pineapples with no bruises or soft spots. Ripe, whole pineapples will stay fresh if stored at room temperature or in the refrigerator for three to four days. This grown-up fruit salad is a tasty addition to a brunch menu.

To remove the skin from a pineapple, trim off the top and bottom so it will sit flat on the cutting board. Using a sharp utility knife, follow the curve of the fruit with the blade of the knife, removing the outer skin. Slice the now-peeled pineapple into the desired thickness. To remove the core and maintain the rings, use a small biscuit cutter or an apple corer.

½	cup honey
	Juice of 2 limes
	Zest of 1 lime
1	teaspoon Grand Marnier or orange liqueur
1	large ripe pineapple, peeled, cored, and cut into 6 pieces
¼	cup chopped fresh mint

- In a large, broiler-proof baking dish combine the honey, lime juice, lime zest, and Grand Marnier. Add the prepared pineapple to the dish and turn to coat. Cover with plastic wrap and let stand at room temperature to marinate at least 1 and up to 2 hours.

- Prepare the grill or broiler to high. Remove the pineapple from marinade, reserving the marinade. Grill or broil the pineapple pieces until golden brown, about 3 minutes per side. Transfer to a serving dish and pour the reserved marinade over the pineapple. Sprinkle with mint and serve immediately.

SOUPS, STEWS & GUMBOS

This chapter will definitely hit home with soup lovers. For those of you who **really** love soup, we once again have some great and easy-to-follow recipes to enjoy no matter what the season. For the readers who feel that soup has its place—you know, the folks who only eat soup when they're sick or whose favorite brand in a can is on sale— I dare you to flip through these pages and try out one of these recipes. I am sure that something's gonna grab you.

As on the show, each recipe will remind you of your own ability to create a fabulous meal. Soups, stews, and gumbos are important foods that few people develop an expertise for. As a result, too many of our first time soup experiences were beef barley, minestrone, or the old standby chicken noodle, all from a can. Hopefully, after reading this you will discover the simplicity of cooking these often undervalued, hearty meals.

POTATO LEEK SOUP

Makes 6 to 8 servings

Potato Leek Soup is a cooking school classic: simple, humble ingredients combined with a few classic techniques. This is a great soup for a cool night. If you want to lighten things up, leave out the milk and cream at the end of cooking since the Yukon Gold potatoes are full of flavor.

Yukon Gold potatoes are medium-size, round potatoes with delicate, yellow-colored skins. Their excellent creamy texture is naturally yellow, giving them a subtle "buttery" flavor. Formerly available only to chefs, Yukon Gold potatoes are now available in most markets and grocery stores for the home cook to enjoy. Yukon Gold potatoes are truly versatile, wonderful for baking, boiling, frying, mashing, and puréeing for soups.

2	bay leaves	4	shallots, diced
3	sprigs fresh rosemary	4	garlic cloves, finely chopped
3	sprigs fresh thyme	2½	pounds Yukon Gold potatoes, peeled and cut into 1-inch pieces
4	sprigs flat-leaf parsley		
1	teaspoon whole black peppercorns	8	cups homemade chicken stock or reduced-fat, low-sodium chicken broth
3	tablespoons olive oil		
4	tablespoons (½ stick) unsalted butter	1	cup milk (optional)
		½	cup heavy cream (optional)
3	celery stalks, finely diced		Coarse salt and freshly ground black pepper
5	leeks, white parts only, well washed and thinly sliced		

- Make a bouquet garni by wrapping the bay leaves, rosemary, thyme, parsley, and peppercorns in cheesecloth and tying it with a piece of kitchen twine.

- Heat the olive oil and butter in a medium stockpot over medium-low heat. Add the celery, leeks, shallots, and garlic. Cook until soft but do not brown, 4 to 5 minutes, stirring occasionally. Add the potatoes, stock, and bouquet garni. Bring the mixture to a boil, and then reduce to a gentle simmer. Cook until the potatoes are tender, about 40 minutes. Remove and discard the bouquet garni.

- Using an immersion blender, purée the soup. Leave it coarse and chunky if you prefer a more rustic soup, or purée it completely smooth for a more elegant soup. (If you don't have an immersion blender, you can purée the soup in a regular blender before pouring back into the pot.) Slowly add the milk and cream, if desired. Return to the saucepan and warm the soup over medium-low heat. Taste and adjust for seasoning with salt and pepper.

SOUTHERN MINESTRONE

Makes 6 servings

Minestrone is a hearty vegetable soup typical of Italian country cooking that contains pasta, such as macaroni, and sometimes peas or beans. This light version uses vegetable stock and is fairly quick cooking, but intensely flavorful.

This one is southern country cooking because of the green beans, yellow squash, zucchini squash, and fresh herbs—often overflowing in summer southern gardens. Free yourself from recipes by understanding how to improvise your own minestrones, depending on what is fresh and available. Country cooks do this all the time; it's the heart of day-to-day home cooking.

2	quarts (8 cups) vegetable stock
¾	cup elbow macaroni
1	(14-ounce) can diced tomatoes, drained
1	cup sliced green beans
1	cup chopped yellow squash
1	cup chopped zucchini squash
1	cup peas, not thawed if frozen
½	cup chopped fresh basil
	Coarse salt and freshly ground black pepper
¼	cup freshly grated Parmigiano-Reggiano cheese

- Bring the stock to a boil in a medium pot over high heat. Add the elbow macaroni. Reduce the heat and simmer until the macaroni is just starting to become tender, about 5 minutes. Add the tomatoes, green beans, and yellow and zucchini squash and stir to combine. Simmer until the macaroni is al dente, about 5 minutes. Add the peas and simmer until heated through, 3 to 5 minutes. Stir in the basil. Taste and adjust for seasoning with salt and pepper. Sprinkle the soup with freshly grated Parmigiano-Reggiano cheese and serve immediately.

OLD-FASHIONED TOMATO SOUP

Makes 4 servings

Tomato soup is the essence of simplicity on its own, but the dish can be enhanced with a number of creative twists. Roasting the tomatoes with a little brown sugar intensifies the flavors. The acidity of the tomatoes combines with the sweetness of the sugar and takes this dish to a whole new level.

This soup is fairly quick and inexpensive, and uses basics in your pantry. Allspice, also known as Jamaican pepper, resembles a blend of cloves, cinnamon, and nutmeg. The pinch of allspice really helps the flavor of the tomato stand out.

2	(28-ounce) cans whole tomatoes, drained, juices reserved	2	tablespoons all-purpose flour
2	tablespoons firmly packed dark brown sugar	1¾	cups homemade chicken stock or reduced-fat, low-sodium chicken broth
4	tablespoons (½ stick) unsalted butter	½	cup heavy cream (optional)
3	large shallots, finely chopped	2	tablespoons brandy or dry sherry
1	tablespoon tomato paste		Coarse salt and freshly ground black pepper
	Pinch of ground allspice		

- Position a rack in the upper third of the oven. Preheat the oven to 450°F. Spray a baking sheet with nonstick spray.

- Working over a strainer set over a medium bowl, open the whole tomatoes and remove the seeds, catching the juices in the bowl. Discard the seeds and reserve the liquid.

- Spread the seeded tomatoes in a single layer on the pan. Sprinkle them evenly with the brown sugar. Bake until all the liquid has evaporated and the tomatoes begin to color, about 30 minutes. Cool slightly and transfer the tomatoes to a small bowl and set aside.

- Heat a large saucepan over medium heat; add the butter. Add the shallots, tomato paste, and allspice. Cook, stirring frequently, until the shallots are softened, 3 to 4 minutes. Add the flour and cook, stirring constantly, until thoroughly combined. Whisking constantly, gradually add the chicken stock. Add the reserved tomato juice and roasted tomatoes, cover, and bring to boil. Reduce heat to simmer and cook, stirring occasionally, about 10 minutes.

- Using an immersion blender, purée the soup. Leave it coarse and chunky if you prefer a more rustic soup or purée it completely smooth for a more elegant soup. Add the cream and heat through, about 3 minutes. Remove the soup from the heat and add brandy. Taste and adjust for seasoning with the salt and pepper, and serve immediately.

DROPPIN' KNOWLEDGE

Finishing soup with cream is a traditional French cooking technique to make the soup smooth and rich. However, you cannot substitute milk for cream as it will curdle. The high fat content of cream coats the proteins and helps prevent curdling. Curdling occurs when proteins join tightly together. This is caused by overheating or a highly acidic environment.

BEEF BARLEY & VEGETABLE SOUP

Makes 8 to 10 servings

Beef and barley soup, sometimes known as Scotch broth, is thick soup made from beef or mutton with vegetables and pearl barley. Barley is an ancient hardy grain. Pearl barley is barley with the bran removed. The bran is the coat of the seed that is broken when the grain is sifted or bolted. Once the bran is steamed, polished, and formed into small grains it resembles pearls. Available in coarse, medium, and fine, pearl barley is a traditional and hearty addition to soups and stews.

Never choose stew meat that is already cut from the butcher's meat case. Not only is it more expensive than cutting up your own, but you have no idea what you might be getting. It could be a mishmash of trimmings. For soups and stews you want beef cut from muscles that do lots of work and get lots of exercise. Work equals flavor. Look for meat from the chuck, which is cut from the shoulder, or round, which is cut from the back legs of the steer. Adding beef bones to the soup will provide intense body and flavor. Any beef bones will do. Ask for bone-in chuck if possible and trim the bone out; otherwise, use trimmed beef ribs or shank.

2	tablespoons vegetable or canola oil
1	pound beef stew meat, such as chuck, round, or bottom round, cut into 1-inch cubes
	Coarse salt and freshly ground black pepper
1	pound beef bones, such as shank
3	carrots, peeled and diced
2	celery stalks, diced
1	large onion, diced
¼	cup pearl barley
4	garlic cloves, finely chopped
4	cups water
3½	cups beef stock or reduced-fat, low-sodium beef broth
1	(28-ounce) can diced tomatoes in juice
1¾	cups fresh corn kernels, about 4 ears
2	cups sliced okra, not defrosted if frozen
2	bay leaves
1½	cups peas, not thawed if frozen

BEEF BARLEY & VEGETABLE SOUP

(continued)

- Heat the oil in a large, heavy-bottom pot over medium-high heat. Season the beef with salt and pepper to taste. Add the stew meat and bones, without crowding, stirring until the beef is well browned on all sides, 8 to 10 minutes. (This may take two batches, depending on the size of your pot.) Transfer the beef and bones to a plate.

- Reduce the heat to medium and add the carrots, celery, onion, and barley. Cook, stirring frequently, until the onion is translucent, 8 to 10 minutes. Add the garlic and cook until fragrant, 45 to 60 seconds. Add the water, beef broth, tomatoes with juices, corn, okra, and bay leaves. Return the beef and bones to the pot and bring to a boil. Season with additional salt and pepper to taste. Reduce the heat to medium low and simmer, uncovered, until the beef is almost tender, 1 to 1½ hours, adding additional water or broth if needed.

- Add the peas, reduce the heat to low, cover, and simmer until heated through, about 5 minutes. Taste and adjust for seasoning with salt and pepper. Serve immediately.

Marvin and country music singer Kelli Coffee taking a break after preparing a mean Birmingham Brunch.

BUTTERNUT SQUASH SOUP

Makes 4 to 6 servings

Squash is usually divided into two categories—summer and winter. Summer squashes are soft and include yellow and zucchini. Winter squash have hard rinds and mature in the fall. Butternut squash is a winter squash. You could also prepare this soup with Carnival, shaped like an acorn squash but with yellow skin with green stripes, or Delicata, shaped like a zucchini and usually yellow with long green stripes. Both are similar in flavor.

Always purchase nutmeg whole so you can grind it yourself for better flavor. This nutty, warm, sweet spice is a common ingredient in beverages, cakes, cookies, and sauces. It also complements the sweet, savory taste of apples, sweet potatoes, and winter squash.

1	plus 1 tablespoon canola oil
1	shallot, finely chopped
3	pounds butternut squash, peeled, seeded, and chopped
3	cups vegetable stock
	Coarse salt and freshly ground black pepper
2	Granny Smith apples, peeled, cored, and diced
1	teaspoon firmly packed dark brown sugar
	Pinch of freshly grated nutmeg

- Heat 1 tablespoon canola oil in a large, heavy-bottom pot over medium-low heat. Add the shallot and cook, stirring frequently, until translucent, about 3 minutes.

- Add the squash and vegetable stock, and bring to a boil. Season with the salt and pepper to taste. Reduce heat to simmer, and cook until the squash is tender, about 30 minutes.

- Meanwhile, heat the remaining 1 tablespoon oil in a medium skillet over medium heat. Add the diced apples and season with salt and pepper. Cook, stirring frequently until tender, about 5 minutes. Set aside and keep warm.

- Using an immersion blender, purée the soup. Leave it coarse and chunky if you prefer a more rustic soup or purée it completely smooth for a more elegant soup. Add the brown sugar and nutmeg. Taste and adjust for seasoning with salt and pepper. Garnish with sautéed apples and serve immediately.

POTATO & CHEDDAR SOUP

Makes 6 servings

Most of us have potatoes, onions, and a hunk of cheese in the house even if the cupboard is otherwise bare, so you could make this delicious soup at a moment's notice.

This is the essence of comfort food—like a loaded baked potato. It's creamy with the tang of the cheese, and freshly snipped chives or scallions add a bit of freshness on top. It's a satisfying meal partnered with a simple salad and some crusty bread.

2	tablespoons vegetable or canola oil
1	onion, chopped
1	carrot, diced
1	celery stalk, diced
2	garlic cloves, finely chopped
1	teaspoon chopped fresh thyme
	Coarse salt and freshly ground black pepper
3	tablespoons all-purpose flour
4	cups homemade chicken stock or reduced-fat, low-sodium chicken broth
3	cups milk, skim, low-fat, or whole
4	large russet potatoes, peeled and diced, about 1¾ pounds
3	cups packed, freshly grated, sharp Cheddar cheese, about 12 ounces
	Hot sauce
	Freshly snipped chives for garnish

- Heat the oil in a large heavy pot over medium heat. Add the onion, carrot, celery, garlic, and thyme. Season with the salt and pepper to taste. Sauté until vegetables begin to soften, 5 to 7 minutes. Sprinkle the flour over the vegetables and cook, stirring, for 2 minutes. Gradually whisk in the stock then the milk. Add the potato and bring the soup to a boil. Reduce the heat and simmer until the potato is tender, about 20 minutes.

- Add the cheese about ⅓ cup at a time, stirring until melted and smooth after each addition. Taste and adjust for seasoning with hot sauce to taste and salt and pepper. Sprinkle with chives and serve immediately.

CRAB BISQUE

Makes 6 servings

This bisque recipe is from the Georgia Gold Coast—pretty fancy eats, but using what the salty southern waters provide us. Blue crabs are harvested from Maryland south through Florida and in parts of the Gulf of Mexico. The eastern seaboard is riddled with shallow, muddy inlets of brackish water where the crabs live.

Bisque is traditionally a rich shellfish soup made with the shells of crab, shrimp, or lobster, and is customarily enriched with cream and Cognac and garnished with pieces of the shellfish. We're taking a little of a shortcut by using already-picked crab. To substitute for the shell stock, use a combination of bottled clam juice and chicken stock. This rich, delicious soup is great for the holidays or a special occasion.

FOR THE STOCK:

1   carrot, coarsely chopped

1   onion, coarsely chopped

1   celery stalk, coarsely chopped

1   teaspoon chopped fresh thyme

1   bay leaf

10   peppercorns

6   cups homemade chicken stock or reduced-fat, low-sodium chicken broth

2   cups fish stock or 2 (8-ounce) bottles clam juice

½   cup dry white wine

FOR THE BISQUE:

¼   cup (4 tablespoons) unsalted butter

1   onion, finely diced

2   carrots, finely diced

2   celery stalks, finely diced

1   garlic clove, finely chopped

1   tablespoon chopped fresh flat-leaf parsley, plus more for garnish

¼   cup all-purpose flour

½   teaspoon chopped fresh thyme

2   tablespoons tomato paste

    Coarse salt and freshly ground black pepper

8   ounces jumbo lump crabmeat, picked over, 6 lump pieces reserved for garnish

⅛   teaspoon cayenne (or to taste)

¼   cup brandy or Cognac

CRAB BISQUE

(continued)

- For the stock, combine the carrot, onion, celery, thyme, bay leaf, peppercorns, chicken stock, clam juice, and white wine in a stockpot over high heat. Bring to a boil and then reduce the heat to simmer. Cook until flavorful and fragrant, about 20 minutes. Strain through a fine-mesh sieve into a large bowl and discard the solids.

- For the bisque, melt the butter in a large pan over medium heat. Add the onion, carrot, and celery and cook, stirring occasionally, until softened and translucent, about 10 minutes. Add the garlic and cook, stirring occasionally, until fragrant, 45 to 50 seconds. Add the parsley, flour, thyme, and tomato paste. Stir to combine. Cook and continue to stir for 1 minute. Stir in the stock and bring to a boil. Season with the salt and pepper to taste. Reduce the heat to medium low and allow the mixture to simmer for about 20 minutes.

- Stir in the crabmeat and cayenne and simmer until heated through, 5 to 7 minutes. Add the brandy and stir to combine. Taste and adjust for seasoning with salt and pepper. Ladle into six rimmed soup bowls. Garnish with reserved crab and parsley and serve immediately.

Marvin giving wife Petra Woods a little one-on-one cooking lesson away from home.

STOVETOP LOW-COUNTRY BOIL

Makes 6 servings

Low-country boils are famous on the coasts of Georgia and South Carolina. Traditionally prepared in a big pot on an outdoor gas cooker, a low-country boil usually contains sausage, shrimp, sometimes crab, potatoes, and corn for an all-in-one pot all-you-can-eat buffet. This version brings the party indoors for every-night cooking.

Here we prepare our own spice blend; store any leftovers in an airtight container up to three months. (It won't be as good, but as a time-saver, you could use a prepared spice blend.) Also, it is very important not to overcook the shrimp; they will get rubbery and tough. Basically, add the shrimp and cook them just until they turn pink. It only takes a few minutes.

¼	cup yellow mustard seeds	¼	cup coarse salt
2	tablespoons black peppercorns	3	pounds red new potatoes, scrubbed clean
1	tablespoon red pepper flakes (or to taste)	1½	pounds smoked spicy sausage, such as andouille or kielbasa, cut into 6 pieces
4	bay leaves		
1	tablespoon celery seeds	6	ears fresh corn on the cob, shucked
1	tablespoon coriander seeds		
1	tablespoon ground ginger	3	pounds large shrimp, unpeeled
¼	teaspoon ground mace		Hot sauce for serving
2	to 3 lemons, halved		

- Combine the mustard seeds, black peppercorns, red pepper flakes, bay leaves, celery seeds, coriander seeds, ginger, and mace in a bowl. Stir to combine. Working in batches if necessary, place the combined spices into a spice grinder and pulse several times until crushed and fragrant.
- Fill a large pot with water (enough to cover all ingredients). For each quart of water, add ½ tablespoon spice mixture and ½ lemon. (Store any leftover spice blend in an airtight container up to three months.)
- Add the salt and potatoes and bring to a boil over high heat. Add the sausage to the boiling water. Reduce the heat to medium and cook for 15 minutes. Add the corn and cook until tender, 8 to 10 minutes. Add the shrimp and cook until pink, about 3 minutes. Drain the mix in a large colander. Transfer the shrimp, sausage, and vegetables to a large platter. Serve immediately with hot sauce and additional halved lemons.

[SEE PHOTO ON PAGE 30]

DROPPIN' KNOWLEDGE

As soon as corn is harvested the sugar starts converting to starch and the corn loses its sweetness. To store corn, leave the husks on, and place it in a damp paper bag inside a plastic bag in the refrigerator. Use it within 24 hours.

TURKEY & BLACK BEAN CHILI

Makes 6 servings

People are generally aware of the healthfulness of turkey. Turkey's versatility makes it ideal as the low-fat alternative to more traditional chili favorites like pork or beef. This heart-healthy chili has lots of garlic and spices. With this much flavor, you won't miss the fat.

Chili powder is a seasoning made from ground, dried chiles, coriander, cumin, garlic, oregano, and other herbs and spices. It can vary in heat from mild to hot. Cooking your own beans is better than using canned, but if you have to use canned as a time-saver, make sure to rinse them in a sieve to remove the "tinny" taste of the can. Feel free to substitute pinto or red beans if you like.

2	tablespoons canola or olive oil	3	cups homemade chicken stock or reduced-fat, low-sodium chicken broth
1	large onion, chopped		
2	red bell peppers, seeded and chopped	1	(28-ounce) can diced tomatoes with juice
6	garlic cloves, finely chopped		Coarse salt and freshly ground pepper
2	pounds ground turkey		
¼	cup tomato paste	1	small red onion, diced for serving
3	tablespoons chili powder		
2	teaspoons ground cumin	1	cup low-fat sour cream for serving
2	teaspoons dried oregano		
3	(15-ounce) cans black beans, rinsed and drained		Hot sauce for serving

- Heat the oil in a large, heavy-bottom pot over medium-high heat. Add the onion, bell peppers, and garlic, and sauté, stirring, until the vegetables begin to soften, 5 to 7 minutes. Add the turkey, and sauté until cooked through, breaking it into small pieces, about 5 minutes. Add the tomato paste, chili powder, cumin, and oregano, and stir to combine.

- Add the beans, chicken stock, and tomatoes with juice, and stir to combine. Bring to a boil, and then reduce the heat to simmer. Cook, uncovered, stirring occasionally, until the chili thickens and the flavors develop, about 1 hour. Taste and adjust for seasoning with salt and pepper. Serve topped with the red onion, sour cream, and plenty of hot sauce on the side.

CHICKEN STEW
WITH TOMATOES & NAVY BEANS

Makes 6 servings

This hearty stew is a convenient dish that freezes and reheats well. The key to achieving the fullest flavor is browning the chicken to a deep golden brown. An improperly heated pan produces chicken with pale, flabby skin. When the pan is heated until the oil smokes, the skin will crisp and brown.

The bacon adds a lot of flavor as well. However, if you wanted to leave it out altogether, substitute about two tablespoons canola oil. Finally, to really cut the fat, you can remove the skin from the chicken after you have seared it.

6	slices bacon, diced	2	cups homemade chicken stock or reduced-fat, low-sodium chicken broth
6	chicken thighs, bone in and skin on, about 2½ pounds		
	Coarse salt and freshly ground black pepper	¾	cup dry red wine
		½	cup chopped fresh basil
	All-purpose flour for dredging	2	tablespoons chopped fresh oregano
1	large onion, chopped		
6	garlic cloves, finely chopped	2	(15-ounce) cans navy beans, rinsed and drained
1	(28-ounce) can whole, stewed tomatoes		

- Heat a large saucepan over medium-high heat. Add the bacon and cook until crisp, stirring occasionally. Using a slotted spoon, transfer the bacon to a plate lined with paper towels to drain.

- Season the chicken with salt and pepper to taste. Dredge the chicken in the flour, shaking to remove the excess. Without crowding add the chicken to the saucepan and sauté until brown, 3 to 5 minutes per side. Transfer the chicken to a medium bowl.

- Remove all but 2 tablespoons drippings from the sauté pan. Reduce the heat to medium; add the onion and sauté until soft and translucent, about 5 minutes. Add the garlic and sauté until fragrant, 45 to 60 seconds.

- Return the cooked and drained bacon and add the stewed tomatoes, chicken stock, and red wine. Bring to a boil, scraping any browned bits on the bottom of the pan. Return the chicken and any accumulated juices. Cover, reduce the heat to low, and simmer until the chicken is tender and the juices of the chicken run clear when pierced with a knife, about 20 minutes.

- Add the basil, oregano, and beans, and simmer 10 minutes longer. Taste and adjust for seasoning with salt and pepper. Serve immediately.

SLOW COOKER BEEF STEW

Makes 6 to 8 servings

Opening the door on a cold night and being greeted by the inviting smells of stew from a slow cooker can be a dream come true. But winter is not the only time a slow cooker is useful. In the summer, using a slow cooker avoids heat from a hot oven—and it takes less electricity.

Slow cookers, also known by the brand name "Crock Pot," cook foods slowly at a low temperature—generally between 170°F and 280°F. The low heat helps less expensive, leaner cuts of meat become tender and shrink less. If you do not have a slow cooker, it's fine to use a heavy-duty pot instead. Of course, you cannot leave it unattended, but the end results will be the same.

1	cup beef stock or reduced-fat, low-sodium beef broth
2	teaspoons Worcestershire sauce
2	garlic cloves, finely chopped
2	teaspoons paprika
2	pounds beef chuck or stew meat, cut into 1½-inch cubes
	Coarse salt and freshly ground black pepper
3	large carrots, diced
3	Idaho potatoes, diced
3	medium onions, quartered
1	celery stalk, diced
2	bay leaves

- Combine the beef stock, Worcestershire sauce, garlic, and paprika in a bowl.

- Season the beef with salt and pepper. Place the carrots, potatoes, onions, celery, and beef in the slow cooker in that order. (The vegetables take longer to cook and need to be on the bottom.) Add the spice mixture and bay leaves. Season with the salt and pepper.

- To complete in a slow cooker: Cover and cook on low for 10 to 12 hours or on high 5 to 6 hours. To complete on the stovetop: Bring the stew to a boil, cover, reduce the heat to simmer, and cook for 2 to 3 hours until the meat is tender. Taste and adjust for seasoning with salt and pepper. Serve immediately.

SEAFOOD GUMBO

Makes 8 to 10 servings

This recipe is great for when you want to get a good bang for your buck. You get a lot of flavor and heartiness, and you don't have to use a lot of pots and pans to achieve a great dish.

The first step is to make your own shrimp stock. It is easy to do and adds a layer of flavor to your gumbo. Peel the shrimp, saving the shells (heads also if you like), and rinse them off with water. Place the shells in a pot and add enough water to cover. Add a few bay leaves, sprigs of parsley and thyme, quartered onion, chopped carrot, chopped celery, and bring to a boil. Reduce the heat to a simmer and cook until fragrant and flavorful, about thirty minutes. Strain the stock in a strainer layered with cheesecloth.

Some gumbos call for okra to flavor and thicken and others call for filé powder. Filé powder is made from the ground dried leaves of the sassafras tree. Stir filé powder into the dish after it has been removed from the heat; otherwise, it will become harsh and chewy.

DROPPIN' KNOWLEDGE

The best way to chop an onion is to top and tail. Start by cutting off both ends. Then cut it in half from top to bottom. Place the cut halves, flat side down, on a work surface. Remove the skin and make vertical cuts lengthwise without cutting all the way through; this holds the onion together as you work. Make a few horizontal cuts from the cut edge toward the root end and then chop across the onion to make cubes.

¾	cup (1½ sticks) unsalted butter
1	cup all-purpose flour
1	large onion, chopped
1	green bell pepper, seeded and chopped
1	red bell pepper, seeded and chopped
2	celery stalks, chopped
3	garlic cloves, finely chopped
5	cups shrimp stock or water
3	bay leaves
3	sprigs fresh thyme, chopped
2	teaspoons hot sauce
	Coarse salt and freshly ground black pepper
1	pound medium-size shrimp, peeled and deveined
1	pound lump crabmeat, picked through for any cartilage and shells
2	dozen freshly shucked oysters, liquid reserved
3	tablespoons chopped fresh parsley
2	scallions, chopped
	Hot, cooked rice for serving
	Filé powder

(continued)

- Heat the butter in a heavy-bottom pot or Dutch oven over medium heat. Add the flour, stirring slowly and constantly to make a medium-brown roux, about 30 minutes. Add the onion and bell peppers, and cook, stirring, until the vegetables are wilted and lightly golden, about 5 minutes. Add the celery and the garlic. Cook, stirring, for 3 minutes. Add the shrimp stock or water, bay leaves, thyme, and hot sauce. Season with salt and pepper to taste. Reduce the heat to medium-low, cover, and simmer for 45 minutes.

- Add the shrimp and crabmeat and simmer until the shrimp turn pink, about 3 minutes. Add the oysters and their liquid and simmer until the edges of the oysters curl, about 2 minutes. Taste and adjust for seasoning with salt and pepper. Garnish with the parsley and scallions. Serve the gumbo over hot, cooked rice. Pass the filé powder separately and serve immediately.

Marvin Cooking up some Hot Buttered Soul
at Club Isaac Hayes.

NEW SOUTHERN CHICKEN & DUMPLINGS

Makes 6 to 8 servings

You may think chicken and dumplings is only an old-fashioned comfort food. We've updated it with skinless, boneless, chicken breasts and given it a little pizzazz with Parmesan cheese and herbed dumplings.

Parmesan is a hard, dry cheese made from cow's milk. The rind is golden tan and the interior is creamy yellow. Parmesan cheeses are made all over the world, but none compares with Italy's Parmigiano-Reggiano, aged eighteen to thirty-six months. Parmigiano-Reggiano is sharp and rich in flavor with a salty kick. Real Italian Parmigiano-Reggiano cheese has Parmigiano-Reggiano stenciled on the rind to authenticate the origin. The cheese is well worth the expense.

6	skinless, boneless chicken breasts		1	large egg, lightly beaten
1	quart (4 cups) homemade chicken stock or reduced-fat, low-sodium chicken broth		$\frac{1}{2}$	cup milk
			2	garlic cloves, peeled and crushed
			1	large onion, diced
FOR THE DUMPLINGS:			4	carrots, peeled and cut $\frac{1}{2}$ inch thick
$1\frac{1}{2}$	cups all-purpose flour		1	pound sweet potatoes, peeled and cut into $\frac{1}{2}$-inch pieces
$\frac{1}{2}$	cup freshly grated Parmigiano-Reggiano cheese		$\frac{1}{4}$	teaspoon red pepper flakes (or to taste)
	Coarse salt and freshly ground black pepper		1	pound Swiss chard, rinsed, stemmed, and cut into $\frac{1}{2}$-inch pieces
2	tablespoons chopped fresh parsley			

- Place the chicken in a stockpot and add chicken stock to cover. Bring to a boil and reduce heat to simmer. Cook until the chicken is tender, 15 to 20 minutes. Remove the chicken with a slotted spoon to a plate to cool slightly, reserving the stock. Cut the chicken into 1-inch chunks.

- Prepare the dumplings: Combine the flour, cheese, salt and pepper to taste, and parsley. Stir in the egg and milk.

- Bring the reserved stock to a boil. Add the chicken, garlic, onion, carrots, sweet potatoes, and red pepper flakes. Reduce the heat to simmer and cook about 10 minutes. Place walnut-size pieces of dough into simmering stock, cover, and continue to simmer until the dumplings are cooked all the way through, an additional 20 minutes. Add the Swiss chard and stir to combine. Cover and cook until wilted, about 5 minutes. Taste and adjust for seasoning with salt and pepper. Serve immediately.

Marvin at our home in Atlanta, Insperience Studio by Whirlpool and Kitchenaid.

SALADS
& SLAWS

Believe it or not, salads and slaws are some of my favorite dishes to make and eat. You can be as creative as you like, or you can just keep it simple. Just take slaw (coleslaw). It comes from a Dutch word meaning "cabbage salad," and traditionally it is made with cabbage and mayonnaise. Y'all know that in the South slaw is crucial to a good meal and is served with everything from barbeque to fried chicken. Heck, it is so intertwined with southern recipes that you would think that it originated in the South. Not so, but the South **has** added a regional aspect to its slaw. In the South not only do you not have to use cabbage, you can skip the mayonnaise as well and still make a mean slaw.

Another one of the joys with salads and slaws is that you can eat them raw or cooked, add protein, make a million types of dressings from mustard to mayonnaise, or leave them undressed. The color scheme is endless, and my rule is the more color the better the taste and the better it is for you. I assure you the following salads won't disappoint you. There are endless choices, creations, and flavors to experience. Did I mention the interchangeable ingredients? Today you can use radicchio and tomorrow use frisée or Swiss chard. I could go on and on, but I won't because I'm sure you would like to get started.

HEIRLOOM TOMATO SALAD
WITH GEORGIA GOAT CHEESE

Makes 6 servings

Heirloom tomatoes come in all kinds of shapes, sizes, colors, and tastes. They are the varieties that have been passed down through the generations from hundreds of farmers and gardeners around the world. If you can't find heirloom tomatoes, this salad would also be delicious with any ripe tomato from your garden or market.

Georgia's family-owned Sweet Grass Dairy makes award-winning artisanal cheeses. Their attitude is: "You simply can't make bad cheese from good milk." It's fantastic we've got such amazing products right here in the South. The goats live outdoors, get exercise, and enjoy grazing in lush pastures. The dairy maintains farming practices that nourish the soil. Fresh goat cheese is also known as chèvre. It should be creamy and smooth with an almost sweet and very floral taste. You can find goat cheese or chèvre at better grocery stores and markets.

1½	tablespoons red wine vinegar
½	teaspoon Dijon mustard
	Coarse salt and freshly ground black pepper
¼	cup extra-virgin olive oil
3	pounds mixed heirloom tomatoes, halved or cut into wedges
4	to 6 ounces goat cheese, crumbled
¼	cup finely chopped fresh mixed herbs such as parsley, basil, and cilantro

- Whisk together the vinegar, mustard, and salt and pepper to taste in a large bowl.
- Add the oil in a slow, steady stream, whisking constantly until the dressing is emulsified. Add the tomatoes and gently toss to coat.
- Add the goat cheese—if very fresh, add teaspoonfuls of the goat cheese—and herbs and toss to coat. Taste and adjust for seasoning with salt and pepper. Serve immediately.

DROPPIN' KNOWLEDGE

Wet and dry measuring cups cannot be used interchangeably. For example, when you measure a dry ingredient such as flour or sugar it should be scooped, leveled, and scraped. A dry measure will work for a wet ingredient, but it is more difficult as dry measures often do not have lips for pouring and it is necessary to fill them to the rim.

MIXED GREENS WITH
HONEY-MUSTARD DRESSING

Makes 4 to 6 servings

Olive oil is a flavorful oil that has been prized for centuries. Now we know it is monounsaturated. Monounsaturated fat is considered to be probably the healthiest type of general fat. It has none of the adverse effects associated with saturated fats, trans fats, or omega-6 polyunsaturated vegetable oils.

The flavor of olive oil is related to the region and climate in which it was produced. Olive oil from Spain tastes different from olive oil produced in Italy. Extra virgin is the highest quality oil. It is cold pressed, using pressure only, with no heat or chemicals. The result is a low-acid, flavorful oil that is the most expensive. It's best used for dipping, drizzling, and making salad dressings.

6	to 8 cups bite-size pieces of salad greens such as iceberg, romaine, and red-leaf lettuce
	Juice of 1 large lemon
1	tablespoon honey
1	teaspoon whole-grain Dijon mustard
1/3	cup extra-virgin olive oil
	Coarse salt and freshly ground black pepper

- Wash the lettuce and spin it dry in a salad spinner. Place it in a large bowl.

- Combine the lemon juice, honey, and mustard in a small bowl. Add the olive oil in a slow, steady stream until the dressing is emulsified. Season with the salt and pepper to taste. Drizzle the honey-mustard dressing over the mixed greens and toss to combine. Taste and adjust for seasoning with salt and pepper. Serve immediately.

CHOPPED SALAD

Makes 6 servings

This is one of those salads where you can put in as many or as few different vegetables as you like and still come up with a great dish. And if you happen to be watching what you are eating these days like most folks, you can just relax and go to town on this one 'cause it is full of color, and I say the more color the better it is for you. Need a new salad to take to a potluck, picnic, or dinner on the grounds? Leave those drippy, mayonnaise-based, layered salads at home. This is the one.

Fennel is also called sweet anise. It has a very mild licorice flavor and is grown throughout the Mediterranean and United States. It grows well here in the sunny South. Fennel has a pale green bulbous base that's used like a vegetable. It can be eaten raw or sautéed or braised. It nicely complements seafood and poultry. If you are fortunate enough to purchase fennel with greenery attached, make sure to use the greenery as a garnish. To slice fennel, trim the root end. Then, halve the bulb and, using a knife, remove the solid white core. Thinly slice into strips and enjoy.

2	hearts of romaine lettuce, chopped	1	(15-ounce) can garbanzo beans (chickpeas), rinsed and drained
6	tablespoons extra virgin olive oil	1	red bell pepper, seeded and diced
2	tablespoons red wine vinegar	1	small red onion, thinly sliced
	Juice of ½ lemon	1	small fennel bulb, cored and thinly sliced
2	teaspoons chopped fresh oregano	4	ounces feta cheese, crumbled
2	garlic cloves, finely chopped	2	ounces salami, thinly sliced and cut into strips
	Coarse salt and freshly ground black pepper	¼	cup kalamata olives, pitted

- Wash the lettuce and spin it dry in a salad spinner. Place it in a large bowl.
- Using a small bowl, whisk together the oil, vinegar, lemon juice, oregano, and garlic. Season with the salt and pepper to taste.
- To the lettuce add the garbanzo beans, bell pepper, red onion, fennel, feta cheese, salami, and olives. Pour the dressing over the salad and toss to combine. Taste and adjust for seasoning with salt and pepper. Serve immediately.

BLACK-EYED PEA SALAD
OVER MIXED GREENS

Makes 6 servings

Black-eyed peas are a southern staple. This is a great recipe to use up leftover peas and give them a fresh taste. It's always best to start from scratch and cook your own beans and peas. If using fresh peas, cook them in boiling, salted water with a little bit of olive oil until just tender. If using dried peas, first pick them clean of rocks and dirt. Soak them in water overnight and then drain. Rinse the peas after soaking, and then use fresh water when you cook them. Place the peas in a pot and add water to cover. Bring to a boil, and then reduce the heat to simmer. Cook until just tender, about one hour. Don't overcook them, or they'll get mushy. If you have to use canned black-eyed peas as a time-saver, first make sure to wash them in a sieve.

Without a doubt, pre-washed organic greens are a definite timesaver for making salads. Different companies make different mixes. Look for crisp, not wilted, greens with no bruises or blemishes. And if they are in a bag, make sure there's no moisture and they are not too wet.

6	to 8 cups mixed greens such as Bibb, radicchio, romaine, mizuna, baby spinach, and beet
½	cup reduced-fat sour cream
⅓	cup apple cider vinegar
2	tablespoons sugar
1	red onion, thinly sliced
½	English cucumber, seeded and thinly sliced
½	red bell pepper, seeded and thinly sliced
1	(15-ounce) can black-eyed peas, rinsed and drained
	Coarse salt and freshly ground black pepper

- Wash the mixed greens and spin them dry in a salad spinner. Place them in a large bowl.
- Whisk together the sour cream, vinegar, and sugar in a medium bowl. Add the onion, cucumber, pepper, and peas. Toss to coat. Season to taste with the salt and pepper. Cover and refrigerate until needed. Serve over the mixed greens.

Dominique Wilkins has dunked on Marvin's
Roasted Red Pepper & Eggplant Dip with Pita Wedges (page 6)

BROCCOLI, VIDALIA ONION & GEORGIA PECAN SALAD

Makes 6 servings

Vidalia onions are no ordinary onions. They have developed an international reputation as the "world's sweetest onion." In one of nature's most delicious mysteries, the very same onion seed will produce a hot onion elsewhere, yet in Georgia it grows into a Vidalia onion one "can eat like an apple." This is due to the unique combination of soils and climate found in the twenty-county production area near Vidalia and Glennville, Georgia.

Dropping a little more knowledge on Georgia agriculture, Georgia leads the nation in pecan production. Pecans provide essential nutrients like oleic acid, which can help lower "bad" (LDL) cholesterol levels, and they are rich in vitamin E, thiamin, magnesium, and copper. This salad is good and good for you.

1	large bunch broccoli, stem ends removed	1	garlic clove, very finely chopped
	Coarse salt		Freshly ground black pepper
½	cup pecan halves, coarsely chopped	1	small Vidalia or sweet onion, thinly sliced
2	tablespoons sugar	1	small red bell pepper, seeded and thinly sliced
¼	cup red wine vinegar		
2	tablespoons extra virgin olive oil		

- Separate the broccoli into florets. Peel and thinly slice the stalks crosswise. Prepare an ice bath and set aside. Bring a large pot of water to a boil. Season with salt and add the broccoli florets. Cook until al dente, or just tender, 2 to 3 minutes. Remove with a slotted spoon and "shock" the broccoli by transferring it to the ice bath to set the color and stop the cooking. Once chilled, remove the broccoli to a plate lined with paper towels. (Do not leave the broccoli in the water or it may become too waterlogged.)

- Preheat the oven to 350°F. Place the chopped pecans on a baking sheet and toast until fragrant, about 5 minutes. Set aside to cool.

- In a small bowl whisk together the sugar and vinegar. Add the olive oil in a slow, steady stream. Add the garlic and season to taste with salt and pepper.

- In a medium bowl combine the broccoli, onion, red pepper, and toasted pecans. Just before serving, drizzle the dressing over the broccoli mixture and toss to combine. Taste and adjust for seasoning with salt and pepper. Serve immediately.

SPINACH, BACON & GOAT CHEESE SALAD WITH GEORGIA PECANS

Makes 6 servings

This is the southern twist on a classic French salad. You will often see this on a restaurant menu, and now you can do it at home. Spinach is an excellent source of vitamin A, folacin, fiber, potassium, and vitamin C. This salad comes together quickly, so have all of the ingredients ready before you start cooking. The prewashed, organic bags of spinach are invaluable. When adding the vinegar to the skillet, step back from the stovetop—the aroma is quite powerful.

People eat bacon less often—and in smaller amounts—in a world that is increasingly health conscious. Bacon is a guilty pleasure, a salty memory of less vigilant times. So, for those special occasions when you do go whole hog, make sure you are getting your money's worth. Buy premium quality bacon with a good balance of meat, salt, and smoke.

½	pound sliced bacon	2	tablespoons cider vinegar
3	tablespoons plus 2 teaspoons olive oil	6	to 8 cups baby spinach
¾	cup pecans	2	ounces goat cheese, crumbled
	Coarse salt and freshly ground black pepper		

- Cook the bacon in a large skillet until crisp, and then transfer with tongs to a plate lined with paper towels to drain. Reserve 2 tablespoons of the rendered fat from the skillet, discarding the remaining fat. Wipe the skillet with a dry paper towel to clean. Once the bacon has cooled, crumble it and set aside.

- Heat 2 teaspoons olive oil in the same skillet over moderate heat. Add the pecans and cook, stirring occasionally, until golden brown and toasted, 3 to 5 minutes. Transfer to a plate lined with paper towels to drain. Once cooled, transfer the pecans to a cutting board. Season with the salt and pepper to taste. Coarsely chop the pecans.

- Heat the reserved 2 tablespoons bacon fat in the skillet over moderately low heat until just warm. Remove the pan from the heat and whisk in the vinegar and the remaining 3 tablespoons olive oil. Season the dressing with salt and pepper to taste.

- Combine the spinach, bacon, goat cheese, and half the toasted pecans. Pour the hot dressing over the spinach mixture. Toss the salad gently with tongs until the spinach is slightly wilted. Taste and adjust for seasoning with salt and pepper. Top with the remaining toasted pecans. Serve immediately.

SPINACH, ORANGE & ALMOND SALAD

Makes 4 to 6 servings

This salad contains both segments of orange and orange zest. Zest is the fragrant, outermost skin layer of citrus fruit and contains the aromatic oils. Only the colored part of the skin, and not the white pith below, is considered the zest.

Tarragon and orange are a natural combination. The herb tarragon has narrow, pointed, dark green leaves and a light anise flavor. Tarragon is widely used in classic French cooking for poultry and seafood dishes and many sauces, including sauce béarnaise. Béarnaise is served with steak au poivre. Tarragon will grow in a southern herb garden in the summer and early fall.

4	oranges	1	medium shallot, finely chopped
⅔	cup sliced almonds, divided	1	tablespoon chopped fresh tarragon
3	tablespoons white wine vinegar		Coarse salt and freshly ground black pepper
1	tablespoon honey		
6	tablespoons olive oil	6	to 8 cups baby spinach

- Use a fine grater or rasp to remove the outer orange zest without any pith. Set aside about 1 to 2 teaspoons. Then, with a sharp knife, slice off the top and bottom so the orange will stand on end. Place the orange on the cutting board. Using a sharp knife and working from top to bottom, remove the peel, pith, and outer membranes from the orange. Carefully cut each segment away from the membranes, collecting the juice and segments in a bowl. Squeeze any remaining juice from the membranes before discarding. Drain the segments, and set aside, reserving ¼ cup of the juice. Repeat sectioning process with the remaining oranges.

- In a large, dry skillet over medium heat toast the almonds, stirring frequently, until golden brown and fragrant, about 5 minutes.

- In a small bowl combine the reserved ¼ cup orange juice, vinegar, and honey. Add the olive oil in a slow, steady stream. Add the shallot, tarragon, and reserved zest. Season with the salt and pepper to taste.

- In a large bowl combine the orange segments, spinach, and half the almonds. Drizzle the dressing over the spinach and toss to combine. Sprinkle with the remaining almonds. Taste and adjust for seasoning with salt and pepper. Serve immediately.

RIBBON VEGETABLE SALAD

Makes 4 to 6 servings

The trick to this salad is that everything is long, thin, and crisp. A Japanese mandoline is a great tool for this simple salad. Japanese mandolines are plastic and less expensive than the French, stainless-steel mandolines. The mandoline is an essential tool in nearly every professional kitchen. Many home cooks are discovering its versatility, and it is becoming a favorite home kitchen tool as well. A mandoline performs tasks nearly impossible to do with a knife or food processor. It is equipped with an extremely sharp, angled, stainless-steel blade, and the cuts can be adjusted from nearly translucent to one-eighth inch thick. So, watch your fingers. You can find both Japanese and French mandolines in finer cookware stores. Otherwise, use a sharp vegetable peeler.

Julienne is a type of cut in which the ingredient to be julienned is cut into very thin, "matchstick" strips usually two to three inches long and about one-eighth inch thick.

2	English cucumbers
3	large carrots
1	large red bell pepper, seeded
4	scallions
	Coarse salt and freshly ground black pepper
2	tablespoons rice wine vinegar
2	tablespoons sesame oil
2	tablespoons extra-virgin olive oil

- Cut the cucumbers in half lengthwise. Using a teaspoon or the curved end of the vegetable peeler, remove the seeds.

- Peel and trim the carrots. Using a vegetable peeler or a mandoline, cut the cucumber halves and carrots lengthwise into paper-thin slices or ribbons.

- Using a chef's knife, cut the pepper and scallions into julienne strips. Place all the vegetables in a medium bowl and season to taste with the salt and pepper. In a small bowl whisk together the vinegar and oils and season with salt and pepper. Pour over the prepared vegetables and toss well to combine. Taste and adjust for seasoning with salt and pepper. Serve immediately.

DROPPIN' KNOWLEDGE

Kosher salt is a mined large coarse-grain salt, not a sea salt, that has no additives. Many chefs like kosher salt for its clean flavor and texture. Its name comes from its use in the preparation of meat according to traditional Jewish dietary regulations. Kosher salts differ from brand to brand in their weights and volumes, but in general, if substituting kosher salt for table salt, use about 50 percent more kosher salt than table salt.

ASPARAGUS & CHICKPEA SALAD

Makes 4 to 6 servings

Asparagus is a long-lived perennial that is grown all over the U.S. but does best in places with sandy soil. It grows throughout the Southeast and is a temperamental, but welcome, addition to the southern garden. Asparagus is one of the first vegetables to pop out of the ground in the spring. It will grow as much as one inch an hour when conditions are right.

Pencil thin or thick and hearty is a matter of personal preference. Regardless of size, when buying it in the grocery store look for asparagus that is firm and bright green with intact tips. Cook it as soon as possible since it deteriorates fairly rapidly. Store it in a plastic bag with a damp paper towel wrapped around the stems. It will last three to four days. Cut off the last inch or two of the stem or wherever it snaps naturally when you bend it near the end. Large asparagus is more mature, less tender, and also needs to be peeled.

3	tablespoons Dijon mustard	1	pound asparagus, trimmed
2	tablespoons balsamic vinegar	2	cups watercress, packed
2	tablespoons mayonnaise	1	(15-ounce) can garbanzo beans (chickpeas), rinsed and drained
	Juice of 1/2 lemon		
2	garlic cloves, very finely chopped	2	tablespoons chopped fresh parsley
3/4	cup extra-virgin olive oil		
	Coarse salt and freshly ground black pepper		

- Combine the mustard, vinegar, mayonnaise, lemon juice, and garlic in a bowl and whisk to combine. Add the olive oil in a slow, steady stream until the dressing is emulsified. Season with the salt and pepper to taste.

- Prepare an ice bath and set it aside. Bring a large pot of water to a boil. Season with salt and add the asparagus. Cook until al dente, about 3 minutes. Remove with a slotted spoon and "shock" the asparagus by transferring it to a bowl of ice water to set the color and stop the cooking. Once chilled, remove to a plate lined with paper towels. Do not leave the asparagus in the water or the stems may become too waterlogged.

- Combine the watercress and garbanzo beans in a bowl. Drizzle a little of the dressing over the mixture and toss to coat and combine. Taste and adjust for seasoning with salt and pepper. Transfer to a serving platter. Top with the blanched asparagus. Sprinkle with the parsley. Pour over the remaining dressing and serve immediately.

WATERCRESS, WALNUT & ROQUEFORT SALAD

Makes 4 servings

This salad is full of flavor. Sharp watercress and Belgian endive, slightly bitter but sweet, caramelized walnuts, and salty blue cheese combine to make a great first course for a special occasion or dinner party.

Roquefort is a blue-veined, smooth, and creamy French sheep's-milk cheese with a strong smell and very pronounced flavor. This is one of the oldest known cheeses, having been produced in the region for almost two thousand years. Only cheeses made according to specific standards of production and matured in the area of Roquefort may be called Roquefort. Similar blue cheeses, no matter how delicious, simply may not be called Roquefort. However, other wonderful blue cheeses to substitute include Maytag Blue produced in the United States, England's Stilton, and Italian Gorgonzola.

¼	cup walnuts	1	tablespoon olive oil
1	tablespoon sugar	1	teaspoon chopped fresh tarragon
	Pinch of salt		Coarse salt and freshly ground black pepper
1	teaspoon plus 2 tablespoons walnut oil		
1	garlic clove, finely chopped	2	Belgian endive
2	teaspoons Dijon mustard	2	bunches watercress
	Juice of ½ lemon	2	ounces Roquefort, crumbled

- To make the caramelized walnuts, preheat the oven to 350°F. Place the nuts on a baking sheet and toast in the oven until golden and fragrant, about 10 minutes.

- Using a medium, heavy-bottom sauté pan over medium heat, add the walnuts, sugar, and salt. Cook, stirring, until the sugar caramelizes and coats the nuts. Add 1 teaspoon walnut oil and stir to combine. Transfer the nuts to a baking sheet and separate with a fork.

- Combine the garlic, mustard, and lemon juice in a small bowl. Add the remaining 2 tablespoons walnut oil and olive oil in a slow stream, whisking until emulsified. Add the tarragon and season with salt and pepper to taste.

- Trim and core the endive. Cut into julienne strips. Remove and discard the coarse stems from the watercress. Toss the watercress and endive with the dressing. Top with the crumbled Roquefort and caramelized walnuts. Taste and adjust for seasoning with salt and pepper. Serve immediately.

FRUIT SALAD WITH HONEY

Makes 6 servings

This salad is perfect for a southern Sunday brunch or luncheon, or as a simple summer dessert when it's too hot to get in the kitchen. The color and flavor of honey differ depending on the nectar source or the blossoms visited by the honeybees. Honey color ranges from nearly colorless to dark brown, and the flavor varies from delectably mild to very strong and bold. Try a mild yet fragrant orange, clover, or alfalfa honey in this light fruit salad.

Use what fruit is flavorful and in season. Sweet peaches, nectarines, or plums would also be good. Make certain to add the banana just before serving or it will darken and discolor.

3	tablespoons honey
	Juice of 1 lemon
1	large orange
1	large Golden Delicious apple, unpeeled, cored, diced
1	pear, unpeeled, cored, diced
1	cup seedless red and green grapes
1	cup strawberries, hulled and halved
1	cup raspberries or blueberries
1	banana, peeled and sliced

- Whisk the honey and lemon juice in a large bowl to blend.
- With a sharp knife, slice off the top and bottom of the orange so it will stand on end. Place the orange on a cutting board. Using a sharp knife, working from top to bottom, remove the peel, pith, and outer membranes from the orange. Carefully cut each segment away from the membranes, collecting the juice and segments in the bowl. Squeeze any remaining juice from membranes before discarding.
- Add the apple, pear, grapes, strawberries, and raspberries or blueberries. Toss gently to coat and combine. Cover and chill in the refrigerator for at least 30 minutes and up to 4 hours. Just before serving, add the banana and toss to combine. Serve immediately.

BROCCOLI & GRAPE-TOMATO SALAD

Makes 4 to 6 servings

Balsamic vinegar is made from Trebbiano grapes. The juice is gently heated and then aged in wooden barrels. Different woods are used and the aging process concentrates the flavors of the vinegar. The result is fragrant, mildly sweet, and rich brown in color. Young vinegar is less expensive and is ideal for marinades. The middle-aged ones, from six to twelve years old, are good to add to sauces or braises at the end of cooking, pasta, or salad dressings. A middle-aged, best quality balsamic vinegar is great for this salad.

The very old vinegar is at least twelve years and up to 150 years old. It can be simply sipped like a good fortified wine at the end of a meal. Sometimes the oldest balsamic vinegar is sparingly drizzled over vanilla ice cream, strawberries and peaches, and ricotta or mascarpone. Don't waste it.

1	large head broccoli
1	pint grape tomatoes, halved
12	kalamata olives, pitted and quartered
	Coarse salt and freshly ground black pepper
1	tablespoon balsamic vinegar
1	tablespoon white wine vinegar
2	garlic cloves, very finely chopped
½	teaspoon red pepper flakes (or to taste)
¼	cup extra-virgin olive oil

- Separate the broccoli into florets. Peel and thinly slice the stalks crosswise. Prepare an ice bath and set aside. Bring a large pot of water to a boil. Season with salt and add the broccoli florets. Cook until al dente or just tender, 2 to 3 minutes. Remove with a slotted spoon and "shock" the broccoli by transferring it to the bowl of ice water to set the color and stop the cooking. Once chilled, remove the broccoli to a plate lined with paper towels. Do not leave the broccoli in the water or it may become too waterlogged.

- Add the tomatoes and olives to the broccoli. Season to taste with the salt and pepper.

- In a small bowl whisk together the balsamic vinegar, white wine vinegar, garlic, and red pepper. Add the olive oil in a slow, steady stream until well blended. Drizzle the dressing over the broccoli and toss to combine. Taste and adjust for seasoning with salt and pepper. Serve hot or at room temperature.

HEART-HEALTHY COLESLAW

Makes 4 servings

Old-fashioned coleslaw usually contains lots of mayonnaise. This spicy, sweet version uses sharp white vinegar instead. This recipe is not only healthier, but also better suited for picnics, dinner on the grounds, or anytime there is a lack of refrigeration. Do not leave salads or sandwiches with meat, eggs, or seafood out of refrigeration more than one hour in the hot sun. Potato, pasta, and vegetable salads such as mayonnaise-based coleslaw are ripe for bacterial growth, too, so follow these rules for these types of salads also.

Sweet and sour, cool and crisp, this slaw is so light and refreshing it makes a great accompaniment to spicy dishes. Try varying the slaw by adding slices of Granny Smith apples to give it a crunchy bite.

½	small cabbage, shredded
1	medium Vidalia onion, chopped
1	carrot, shredded
½	small red bell pepper, seeded and chopped
½	small yellow bell pepper, seeded and chopped
¼	cup sugar
¼	cup white vinegar
¼	cup canola oil
½	teaspoon celery seeds
¼	teaspoon mustard seeds
	Coarse salt and freshly ground black pepper

- Combine in a large bowl the cabbage, onion, carrot, and bell peppers. Stir to combine.
- In a medium saucepan over medium heat combine the sugar, vinegar, canola oil, celery seeds, and mustard seeds. Stir until the sugar dissolves. Pour the vinegar mixture over the cabbage mixture and toss gently to combine. Season with the salt and pepper to taste. Cover and chill in the refrigerator for at least 2 hours before serving. Taste and adjust with salt and pepper. Serve immediately.

FENNEL SLAW

Makes 4 to 6 servings

The southern barbecue experience often involves slaw or coleslaw. There are three kinds of slaw: barbecue slaw, coleslaw, and yellow or mustard slaw. Barbecue slaw is chopped cabbage with vinegar and red pepper. It is a western North Carolina barbecue tradition. Coleslaw, also known as white or mayonnaise slaw, is what most people think of when they think of slaw. White slaw is made primarily of cabbage and mayonnaise. Yellow or mustard slaw is more commonly found in South Carolina or eastern North Carolina. As the name implies, it is made with mustard.

Fennel has a light licorice flavor that's crisp and fresh. Our fennel slaw is pretty fancy stuff, definitely high cotton. It's fine to serve at home or to take to a fancy picnic, but do yourself a favor and leave it at home when you're down at the pit.

½	cup mayonnaise
2	tablespoons apple cider vinegar
	Juice of ½ lemon
	Zest of ½ lemon
2	tablespoons chopped fresh dill
2	teaspoons sugar
	Coarse salt and freshly ground black pepper
1½	pounds fresh fennel bulbs, cored, trimmed, and thinly sliced

- Using a large bowl whisk together the mayonnaise, vinegar, lemon juice, lemon zest, dill, and sugar. Season to taste with the salt and pepper. Add the thinly sliced fennel and toss to coat. Cover and chill up to 1 hour. Taste and adjust for seasoning with salt and pepper. Toss again before serving immediately.

[SEE PHOTO ON PAGE 50]

CARROT-APPLE SLAW

Makes 4 to 6 servings

In this Indian-inspired slaw with raisins and cumin, nonfat yogurt takes the place of mayonnaise. And for sweetness, there is apple juice instead of sugar. This heart-healthy side dish goes well with the Turkey and Black Bean Chili (page 43), simply grilled chicken, or pork tenderloin.

Cumin is often used in Latin American, Asian, and Middle Eastern cooking. It is available in both seed and ground forms. It's always better to grind your own spices. Who knows how long those spices have been on the grocery store shelf? As with all seeds, herbs, and spices, cumin should be stored in a cool, dark place for no more than three months.

1	cup plain nonfat yogurt
2	tablespoons golden raisins
¼	cup boiling water
2	tablespoons apple juice
¼	teaspoon ground cumin
4	large carrots, coarsely shredded
2	medium Golden Delicious apples, unpeeled, cored, and coarsely shredded
3	tablespoons chopped fresh parsley
	Coarse salt and freshly ground black pepper

- Line a small, fine-mesh strainer with cheesecloth and place it over a small bowl. Spoon in the yogurt to drain until slightly firm, at least 15 minutes and up to 30. Remove and discard the liquid that collects in the bowl.

- Meanwhile, place the raisins in a small, heatproof bowl or cup and pour the boiling water over them. Set aside to plump about 10 minutes. Drain the raisins, discarding the water.

- In a large bowl combine the drained yogurt with the apple juice and cumin. Add the carrots, apples, parsley, and drained raisins. Toss well to combine and coat. Taste and adjust for seasoning with salt and pepper. Serve immediately.

NAPA CABBAGE SLAW

Makes 6 servings

We love slaw so much in the South, you know every now and then you have to mix things up. This recipe has an Asian kick for a great change of pace. Napa cabbage is also known as Chinese cabbage. It has an oblong head with tightly packed, pale green to white crinkled leaves. Napa has crispy, fibrous leaves with a mild, sweet flavor. It's mild flavor is similar to a cross between cabbage, iceberg lettuce, and celery. It is a versatile cabbage that can be eaten raw or cooked and is used in stir-fry and soups. Fresh Napa cabbage will keep a week or more.

Late in the seventeenth and eighteenth centuries, slaves brought the sesame seed to America. In some parts of the South sesame seeds are known as "benne seeds," which was their name in the African dialect. Sesame seeds have a mild, nut-like flavor, which is intensified when toasted. To toast sesame seeds heat them in a skillet over medium heat, shaking the pan occasionally, until they darken and become fragrant, three to five minutes.

2	tablespoons mayonnaise
2	teaspoons rice vinegar
1	teaspoon Asian sesame oil
1	teaspoon honey
1	medium head Napa cabbage, shredded, about 2 cups
2	carrots, grated
2	scallions, thinly sliced
1	red bell pepper, seeded and thinly sliced
	Coarse salt and freshly ground black pepper
1	tablespoon sesame seeds, toasted

- In a large bowl whisk together the mayonnaise, rice vinegar, Asian sesame oil, and honey. Add the cabbage, carrots, scallions, and red bell pepper. Season with salt and pepper to taste. Toss the vegetables to coat. Sprinkle with sesame seeds. Serve immediately.

SPICY VEGETABLE SLAW

Makes 6 servings

This is a great mix with lots of vegetables—a little sweet, a little sour, and a serious bite of hot sauce. Use whatever cabbage looks and tastes best, although a mix is best for color. Savoy cabbage is like ordinary cabbage, but with a milder flavor.

There's not much worse than a bland, mealy tomato. When tomatoes aren't in season, reach for grape tomatoes. Grape tomatoes contain more sugar than cherry tomatoes and are sweeter. They are a tasty, fast finger-food and they're kid-friendly. Grape tomatoes have a long shelf life, and unlike most cherry tomatoes, can be eaten neatly in one bite, making them a "squirt-free" alternative.

¾	cup reduced-fat mayonnaise
¼	cup cider vinegar
¼	cup sugar (or to taste)
2	teaspoons hot sauce (or to taste)
	Coarse salt and freshly ground black pepper
2	pounds (about 7 cups) mixed cabbages such as green, red, or Savoy, cored and thinly sliced
½	pint grape tomatoes, halved
1	small red onion, thinly sliced
1	cucumber, peeled, seeded, and diced
1	small yellow bell pepper, seeded and thinly sliced

- Using a large bowl whisk together the mayonnaise, vinegar, sugar, and hot sauce until the sugar is dissolved. Season with the salt and pepper to taste.

- Add the cabbage, tomatoes, red onion, cucumber, and yellow bell pepper. Toss to combine and coat. Cover and chill until serving, at least 30 minutes and up to 1 hour. Taste and adjust for seasoning with salt and pepper. Serve immediately.

CORNBREADS
& BREADS

You've come along way, Cornbread! Cornbread has really evolved since first coming on the scene. Just as it sounds, it's made from dried ground corn or cornmeal. As a staple crop of the South, corn has been used historically in a wide variety of foods. Before folks knew what a leavening agent was, corn was used in griddle cornbread and griddle Johnnycakes. And cooked ground corn, with a leavening agent or without, has always been a filling side dish. The same can be said for flour-based foods like dumplings or pasta. Flour has always been plentiful and versatile. It's one ingredient that almost everyone has on the counter or in their refrigerator regardless of how much time they spend cooking. For these reasons, and because they can also be very filling, biscuits rank right up there with cornbread as a southern favorite. While everyone has a little something they do differently with their biscuits, here's a hint to help you judge how yours turned out: if your family uses the gravy you made to go with the meat and potatoes for dipping your biscuits, you did a good job!

BACON CORNBREAD

Makes 1 (10-inch) round loaf

Cast iron is great for baking cornbread, pan-frying, and sautéing meats and vegetables. It's slow to heat up, but once it does, it heats evenly and stays hot longer than other pans. Cast iron is inexpensive and can be found at most hardware and cookware stores.

When properly seasoned over time, cast iron becomes virtually a non-stick surface, which only improves with use. To clean, wipe it with a soft cloth or paper towel. Use soap and water only if absolutely necessary. Before storing, make sure it is completely dry to prevent rust.

½   pound bacon, coarsely chopped
2   cups white cornmeal
1   teaspoon salt
½   teaspoon baking soda
½   teaspoon baking powder
1½ cups buttermilk
1   large egg, lightly beaten

- Preheat the oven to 400°F. In a 10-inch round, cast-iron skillet over medium-high heat, cook the bacon until brown and crisp. Using a slotted spoon, transfer the bacon to a plate lined with paper towels to drain.

- Pour off the drippings and reserve. Return 2 tablespoons drippings to the skillet and set aside ¼ cup for the batter. Reserve any remaining drippings for another use. Place the skillet in the oven to heat.

- In a medium bowl whisk together the cornmeal, salt, baking soda, and baking powder.

- Add the buttermilk, egg, and the ¼ cup reserved drippings. Whisk until just blended. Add the bacon and stir to combine. Pour the batter into the hot skillet. Bake until firm to the touch and golden brown, about 20 minutes. Invert onto a wire rack to cool. Serve immediately.

DROPPIN' KNOWLEDGE

If a recipe calls for buttermilk, it can simply be made by adding 1 tablespoon of white vinegar plus enough milk to equal 1 cup.

CHEDDAR CORNBREAD

Makes 6 servings

There are a lot of cornmeal products on southern grocery shelves—various textures, blends, and colors. It can be confusing. To start, yellow cornmeal is made from yellow corn and white cornmeal is made from white corn. However, they are not always interchangeable.

Self-rising cornmeal has leavening, salt, and is enriched with B vitamins. It does not contain flour. Self-rising cornmeal mix is cornmeal blended with flour, leavening, and salt, and is also enriched with B vitamins. Be certain to read your recipe and make your purchase carefully since cornmeal, self-rising cornmeal, and self-rising cornmeal mix are not at all interchangeable.

1	cup all-purpose flour
1	cup yellow cornmeal
3	teaspoons sugar
1½	teaspoons baking powder
1½	teaspoons baking soda
¾	teaspoon salt
1	cup grated extra-sharp Cheddar cheese, about 4 ounces
1¼	cups buttermilk
2	large eggs, lightly beaten
¼	cup (½ stick) unsalted butter, melted and cooled, plus more for pan

- Preheat the oven to 400°F. Butter an 8 x 8 x 2-inch square baking dish or a medium cast-iron skillet.

- Using a medium bowl whisk together the flour, cornmeal, sugar, baking powder, baking soda, and salt. Stir in the cheese. In a separate medium bowl, whisk together the buttermilk, eggs, and melted butter. Add the buttermilk mixture to the dry ingredients and stir until just combined.

- Pour the batter into the prepared pan. Bake until a cake tester inserted into the center comes out clean and the bread is golden brown, 20 to 25 minutes. Serve warm or at room temperature.

CORN CAKES

Makes about 8 cakes

Corn cakes, corn muffins, corn sticks, corn pone, hoecakes, and johnnycakes are all "pocket breads" that travel well. The word *johnnycake* actually may be a corruption of the term *journey cake*. Early colonists, slaves, poor people, and Native American Indians most likely combined a simple mixture of ground corn, water, and, perhaps, a little salt for their corn cakes.

These cakes eventually evolved as southerners became more prosperous and enriched them with a leavener and egg. Serve these cakes made with fresh corn with soup or stew for a hearty meal.

3	ears corn
1	large egg, lightly beaten
3	tablespoons all-purpose flour
1	tablespoon sugar
1	teaspoon baking powder
	Coarse salt and freshly ground black pepper
1	plus 1 tablespoons canola oil

- Using the largest holes of a grater, grate the corn over a large bowl, yielding about ½ cup. Add the egg and whisk to combine. Stir in the flour, sugar, and baking powder. Season with the salt and pepper to taste.

- Heat 1 tablespoon oil in a heavy-bottom sauté pan or cast-iron skillet over medium-low heat. Working in batches, drop 2 tablespoons batter for each cake. Cook until golden brown, about 2 minutes on each side. Transfer to a plate lined with paper towels. Repeat the process with the remaining oil and batter. Serve immediately.

[SEE PHOTO ON PAGE 72]

*Post crawfish crawl with director Tom Williams, Marvin,
country singer Tracy Byrd, executive producer Mike Thomas,
coauthor and producer Virginia Willis.*

FIESTA CORN MUFFINS

Makes 12 muffins

These corn muffins are a type of quick bread, meaning they use baking powder as a leavener, not yeast. Baking powder is a combination of an acid and bicarbonate of soda (baking soda) that forms the gas that enables baked products to rise. The most common form of baking powder is the double-acting variety, which produces gas upon mixing and again with the heat of the oven.

Buy baking powder in small containers and store it tightly sealed. To test whether baking powder has lost its oomph, place one-half teaspoon into a glass of warm water. If it foams to the top, the baking powder is still active.

1½	cups all-purpose flour
¾	cup yellow cornmeal
¼	cup finely diced red bell pepper
2	tablespoons finely diced sun-dried tomatoes
1	tablespoon baking powder
1	teaspoon ground cumin
¼	teaspoon cayenne (or to taste)
½	teaspoon salt
2	eggs
1	cup milk
⅓	cup vegetable oil, plus more for the pan
¼	cup shredded sharp Cheddar cheese

- Preheat the oven to 425°F. Heavily grease a 12-cup muffin tin.
- In a medium-size mixing bowl whisk together the flour, cornmeal, bell pepper, sun-dried tomatoes, baking powder, cumin, cayenne, and salt.
- In a separate bowl, whisk together the eggs, milk, and oil. Add to the dry ingredients, stirring until just blended. Fill the prepared muffin tin about two-thirds full. Sprinkle the cheese atop the muffins and bake until golden brown, 18 to 22 minutes. Remove to a rack to cool slightly before turning out. Serve immediately.

[SEE PHOTO ON PAGE 72]

BUTTERMILK BISCUITS

Makes 9 (2 to 3-inch) biscuits

The exterior of the perfect biscuit is golden brown and slightly crisp. Straight from the oven, the hot, steaming interior should be light and airy. When making biscuits, it's important to avoid overworking the dough. Overworked dough means a tough biscuit.

A very hot oven is essential. When the butter melts, it produces steam. The steam interacts with the baking powder, and the result is a tender, light, and fluffy biscuit.

2	cups all-purpose flour, or cake flour (not self-rising), plus more for your hands
1	tablespoon baking powder
1	teaspoon salt
4	tablespoons ($\frac{1}{2}$ stick) cold, unsalted butter, cut into cubes
$\frac{3}{4}$	to 1 cup buttermilk

- Preheat the oven to 500°F. Combine the flour, baking powder, and salt in a large bowl. With a pastry cutter or two knives, cut the butter into the flour mixture until it resembles coarse meal. Pour in the buttermilk, and gently mix until just combined. Flour your hands and gently form the mixture into balls.

- Flatten slightly and place in a round 8 x 2-inch cake pan or on a baking sheet. If the biscuits are baked close together, the sides will be moist. If the biscuits are baked farther apart, the sides will be crisp.

- Bake until golden brown, 8 to 10 minutes. Allow to cool to the touch and serve immediately.

ANGEL BISCUITS

Makes about 24

Angel Biscuits are lighter than most because they have yeast in the dough. Most biscuits contain baking powder, baking soda, or a combination of both. A benefit to this recipe is that it can be held in the refrigerator overnight and baked the next day.

Yeast is important to breadmaking because the carbon dioxide produced by yeast is how certain doughs rise. Yeast is a living microscopic, single-cell organism. As it grows and ferments it converts its food into alcohol and carbon dioxide. To accomplish this yeast simply needs a warm, moist environment with something to eat, usually in the form of sugar or starch. These biscuits are as light as air!

½	cup warm water, 105°F to 115°F
1	package active dry yeast, about 2¼ teaspoons
5	cups all-purpose flour, plus more for rolling
¼	cup sugar
1¼	teaspoons salt
1	teaspoon baking powder
1	teaspoon baking soda
½	cup (1 stick) unsalted butter, chilled, cut into ½-inch pieces, plus more for pan and brushing
2	cups buttermilk

- Place the warm water in a small bowl. Sprinkle the yeast over the water to dissolve and set aside for 5 minutes. (This is known as "proofing" and proves that the yeast is still alive.)

- Combine the flour, sugar, salt, baking powder, and baking soda in a large bowl. Using a pastry blender or two knives, cut in the butter until the mixture resembles coarse meal.

- Add the yeast mixture and buttermilk, and stir until just moist. Cover and refrigerate at least 1 hour or overnight.

- Preheat the oven to 375°F. Lightly butter a baking sheet. Remove the dough to a clean, floured surface and punch down. Knead into a ball until smooth, about 5 times. Using a lightly floured rolling pin, roll the dough to a ½-inch thickness. Using a 2½-inch round cutter, cut out the biscuits and place them on the prepared baking sheet. Gently reroll the remaining dough as needed. Brush the tops with melted butter. Bake until golden brown, 12 to 14 minutes. Remove to a rack to cool slightly. Serve immediately.

[SEE PHOTO ON PAGE 72]

VEGETABLE SIDES

It wasn't until I went to culinary school that I learned that vegetables were quick to make and could actually taste good. Learning to blanch and shock and then toss vegetables in, say, some garlic or perhaps shallots with some olive oil, was like learning a magic trick. Now you might not have gone to culinary school and might have missed every helpful cooking lesson about vegetables shown on television or suggested in a book but fret not! I'm here to show you recipes you'll be happy you tried.

Mastering the art of preparing tasty vegetables has become even more important since more and more people are realizing the value of a balanced diet. If you're like me, you've probably had one or two scary vegetable experiences, but now that you have these magical tips your vegetable dishes will evolve into a work of art.

SLOW COOKER BAKED BEANS

Makes 6 to 8 servings

Beans are low in fat and loaded with nutrients—and not very polite flatulence-producing enzymes. To avoid this delicate situation change the water from time to time while you're soaking the beans. Pouring off the water helps get rid of the indigestible complex sugars that will eventually create gas in your intestines. It also helps to cook the beans very thoroughly, until they can be easily mashed with a fork.

Navy beans are commonly used to make baked beans, but they're also good in soups, salads, and chili. A handy guide for cooking most beans is one pound of dried beans equals about two cups dried beans and produces four to five cups of cooked beans.

3	cups dried white navy beans, soaked overnight
1½	cups ketchup
1½	cups water
¼	cup molasses
1	large onion, chopped
1	tablespoon dry mustard
6	slices bacon, chopped
1	cup firmly packed brown sugar
	Coarse salt and freshly ground pepper

- Rinse and drain the beans and place them in the insert of the slow cooker. Add the ketchup, water, molasses, onion, mustard, bacon, brown sugar, and salt and pepper to taste. Stir to combine. To complete in a slow cooker, cover and cook on low for 8 to 10 hours or on high 4 to 5 hours. Taste and adjust for seasoning with salt and pepper. Serve immediately.

BROCCOLI WITH OLIVE OIL, GARLIC & LEMON

Makes 4 to 6 servings

Garlic-infused oil is a little something simple to jazz up an every-night side dish. This broccoli recipe takes just two steps: blanching the broccoli and making the oil. Don't cook the broccoli in lemon juice or the acid will turn the broccoli brown.

When making the paste, it is important the garlic be mashed to a paste. Garlic paste has an even finer texture than minced garlic. To make the paste, place the side of a chef's knife on the garlic clove and give the knife a quick whack with the heel of your hand. Remove the garlic skin. Trim the tiny root and place the garlic on the cutting board. Give it a few chops and then sprinkle it with salt. (The salt acts as an abrasive and helps chop the garlic.) Continue chopping. Then, using the side of the chef's knife like a palate knife, press firmly on the knife and crush the garlic, a little bit at a time.

1	large head broccoli
	Coarse salt
2	tablespoons olive oil
2	garlic cloves, mashed to a paste
	Juice of ½ lemon
	Zest of ½ lemon
	Coarse salt and freshly ground black pepper

- Discard the tough lower third of broccoli stem. Peel the remaining stem and cut crosswise into ¼-inch-thick slices. Divide the broccoli into florets. Bring a large pot of water to a boil. Season with salt and add the broccoli. Cook until al dente, about 3 minutes. Remove with a slotted spoon and place the broccoli in a bowl.

- In a small sauté pan over medium heat put the oil, garlic, lemon juice, and zest. Season with the salt and pepper to taste. Heat the garlic mixture just until fragrant, 45 to 60 seconds. Drizzle the oil over the broccoli and toss to coat and combine. Taste and adjust for seasoning with salt and pepper. Serve immediately.

GARLIC-SESAME BROCCOLI & SPINACH

Makes 4 servings

This colorful side dish is packed full of nutrients. It's also packed with flavor and is certain to shake up the menu. Serve this with grilled chicken or broiled fish for a simple supper. The sesame oil and seeds are what really make the flavors pop.

Sesame oil is amber-colored and richly aromatic. It is made from roasted sesame seeds. Dark or unrefined sesame oil burns easily and loses flavor when overheated, so it is used mostly as a condiment or flavoring for dressings, soups, and stir-fries. It is available at Asian groceries and well-stocked grocery stores.

2	tablespoons olive oil
1	head broccoli cut into 1-inch florets
1	red bell pepper, seeded and diced
2	garlic cloves, finely chopped
¼	teaspoon red pepper flakes (or to taste)
10	ounces fresh spinach
2	teaspoons sesame oil
1	tablespoon sesame seeds
	Coarse salt and freshly ground black pepper

- Heat a large sauté pan over medium-high heat. Add the olive oil and heat until hot, but not smoking. Add the broccoli and red bell pepper. Cook, stirring occasionally, until the broccoli is crisp-tender, 6 to 8 minutes.

- Add the garlic and red pepper flakes. Cook until fragrant, 45 to 60 seconds. Add the spinach and toss to coat. Cover and cook, stirring, until the spinach is just wilted, 1 to 2 minutes. Add the sesame oil and seeds and toss to coat. Taste and adjust for seasoning with the salt and pepper. Serve immediately.

[SEE PHOTO ON PAGE 150]

CORN WITH CAYENNE & PARMESAN

Not much is better on this earth than fresh sweet corn. In the South we are blessed with long, hot summers that produce delicious corn. Corn is the only grain that's commonly eaten as a fresh vegetable and is a great source of vitamin A, fiber, and other nutrients.

It's not unusual to see people peeling back husks in search of ears with perfect rows of kernels. Don't do that. Crooked rows taste just as good as straight. Just take a peek to make sure the ear is full and free of worms, but keeping the husk on helps the corn stay moist and sweet. Freshness is important because the sugars in corn begin converting into starch the moment the corn is picked. Straight from the row to a pot of boiling water is the best.

4	ears corn, not shucked
	Unsalted butter
½	cup freshly grated Parmigiano-Reggiano cheese
	Coarse salt and cayenne

- Preheat the oven to 350°F. Soak the corn in its husk in water to cover for about 30 minutes. Pull the husks back and scrub the silks from the corn. Place the corn in the oven directly on the rack and cook until the corn is tender, 40 to 45 minutes.

- Remove from the heat and shuck to remove the husks. Spread the butter up and down the hot ear of corn to melt and evenly distribute the butter.

- Sprinkle with the Parmigiano-Reggiano cheese, salt, and cayenne. Serve immediately.

CORN SPOON BREAD

Makes 8 servings

Spoon bread is a southern, custard-style cornbread. It's more pudding-like than bread and is baked in a casserole dish. Spoon bread is generally served as a side dish and, in fact, is soft enough that it must be eaten with a spoon or fork. Adding a bit of fresh corn really makes this spoon bread delicious.

It's easier to separate eggs when they are cold; the whites and yolks are firmer and less likely to break. When separating eggs, crack one egg at a time into a cup, transferring each white to the mixing bowl only after it is successfully separated. And, even though it is best to separate eggs when they are cold, egg whites will whip to greater volume when they've had a chance to warm slightly. So, let the egg whites stand at room temperature in the mixing bowl while you assemble the remaining ingredients.

4	cups milk
1¼	cups cornmeal
1½	teaspoons salt
1	cup fresh corn kernels, about 2 ears
2	scallions, chopped
¼	cup (½ stick) unsalted butter, cut into small pieces, plus more for pan
	Coarse salt and freshly ground black pepper
3	large eggs, separated

- Preheat the oven to 375°F. Butter an 8 x 8 x 2-inch baking dish.
- In a medium saucepan over medium heat whisk together the milk, cornmeal, and salt. Bring the mixture to a boil, whisking constantly until the mixture thickens, about 4 minutes. Reduce the heat to low and cook until the mixture is very thick, stirring often, about 20 minutes.
- Transfer the mixture to a large bowl. Add the corn, scallions, and butter. Season with the coarse salt and pepper to taste and stir to combine. Add the egg yolks, one at a time, stirring after each addition.
- In a separate medium bowl using a handheld mixer, beat the egg whites with a pinch of salt until stiff peaks form. Fold the egg whites into the warm cornmeal mixture in two additions.
- Transfer the batter to the prepared pan, using a spatula to smooth the surface. Bake until golden brown, about 30 minutes. Serve immediately.

DROPPIN' KNOWLEDGE

To measure dry ingredients, scoop the ingredient into a dry measuring cup. Do not pack the ingredient into the cup. Using the back of a knife or a straight edge spatula tap across the cup to settle the ingredient then pull the edge straight across the cup to level it.

BROILED TOMATOES STUFFED WITH CORNBREAD

Makes 8 servings

This is a great use for leftover cornbread. Use the ripest tomatoes you can find, but even not-so-great tomatoes benefit from this recipe. Mix it up; try different herbs such as parsley or basil, and add a bit of freshly grated Parmesan cheese.

Fresh from your garden or the market, tomatoes are low-calorie, low-sodium, a good source of fiber, and high in vitamins A and C. Studies show that the antioxidant lycopene found in tomatoes blocks cancer, aging, and cellular damage.

4	large ripe tomatoes
2	cups crumbled cornbread
½	cup mayonnaise
6	slices bacon, cooked crisply and crumbled
2	scallions, chopped
2	sprigs fresh thyme, chopped
	Coarse salt and freshly ground black pepper

- Preheat the oven to 350°F. Halve the tomatoes horizontally with a serrated knife. Using a metal spoon, carefully scoop out the pulp and reserve.
- In a small bowl combine the reserved tomato pulp, cornbread, mayonnaise, bacon, scallions, and thyme. Season with the salt and pepper to taste.
- Spray a glass baking dish with vegetable cooking spray. Spoon the mixture into the tomato shells. Transfer the stuffed tomatoes to the prepared baking dish. Cook until heated through, about 20 minutes. Serve immediately.

[SEE PHOTO ON PAGE 82]

OKRA & TOMATOES

Makes 6 servings

People either love okra or they hate it. Those that hate it think it's slimy. There are a couple of techniques that prevent okra from becoming too slimy. First, do not overcook it. When okra is just cooked, it is fresh and crisp. The other technique is to cook the okra with an acid. This recipe uses tomato as well as a bit of red wine.

Look for okra that is firm and pale green and under four inches long. Any larger and the pods will be tough and inedible. Make sure to buy okra that is not bruised, limp, or starting to discolor. To keep okra in the refrigerator, store it in a paper bag no more than two to three days.

3	tablespoons olive oil
1	medium onion, chopped
2	garlic cloves, finely chopped
½	cup dry red wine
1½	pounds okra, stems trimmed, cut into ½-inch pieces
4	large tomatoes, chopped
3	sprigs fresh thyme
2	bay leaves
	Coarse salt and freshly ground black pepper

- Heat the oil in a sauté pan over medium heat. Add the onion and cook, stirring until translucent, about 5 minutes. Add the garlic and cook until fragrant, 45 to 60 seconds. Add the red wine and cook until reduced by half.

- Add the okra, tomatoes, thyme, and bay leaves. Season with the salt and pepper to taste. Cover and reduce the heat to a low simmer. Cook, stirring occasionally, until the vegetables are fork-tender, about 15 minutes. Taste and adjust for seasoning with salt and pepper. Serve immediately.

TOMATO FLORENTINE

Makes 4 servings

A well-stocked pantry is like a box full of surprises. Fresh is better, but canned doesn't have to mean bland. This recipe uses canned tomatoes. Canned tomatoes aren't actually all that bad. Fresh, vine-ripe tomatoes are amazing, but you can find them only a few months of the year. All too often, tomatoes at the market are mealy and tasteless. Canned tomatoes are consistent and a good product to keep in your cupboard.

Florentine refers to dishes that contain spinach. Also, a Florentine dish is sometimes sprinkled with cheese and browned lightly in the oven.

1	(28-ounce) can whole tomatoes, drained and coarsely chopped
¼	cup freshly grated Parmigiano-Reggiano cheese
1	plus 1 tablespoons olive oil
2	tablespoons panko (Japanese breadcrumbs) or dry breadcrumbs
1	medium onion, chopped
4	garlic cloves, finely chopped
10	ounces frozen chopped spinach, thawed, squeezed, and drained
⅛	teaspoon freshly ground nutmeg
	Coarse salt and freshly ground black pepper

- Preheat the oven to 400°F. Place the tomatoes in a 9-inch square baking dish.

- In a small bowl combine the cheese, 1 tablespoon olive oil, and breadcrumbs.

- Heat the remaining 1 tablespoon olive oil in a medium sauté pan over medium heat. Add the onion and cook until softened, about 5 minutes. Add the garlic and cook until fragrant, 45 to 60 seconds. Add the spinach and stir to combine. Cook, stirring, until heated through, about 2 minutes.

- Remove the pan from the heat. Add the nutmeg and season with salt and pepper to taste. Spoon the spinach mixture evenly over the tomatoes. Sprinkle with the breadcrumb mixture. Transfer to the oven and bake until golden brown, 15 to 20 minutes. Serve immediately.

GREEN BEANS WITH DIJON MUSTARD

Makes 4 servings

Haricot vert is the French term for green beans. *Haricot* means "bean" and *vert* means "green." They are much thinner than regular green beans and often have a better flavor. They are also known as French green beans or French beans. Substitute other thin green beans, but stay away from string beans since they have a tough, fibrous string.

It's best to use good quality Dijon mustard for this dish since there are so few components. Mustard decreases in potency over time, so purchase small jars and replace them frequently. Also, keep mustard in the refrigerator to help keep it fresh.

1	pound haricot vert or other thin green beans, stems trimmed
1	tablespoon olive oil
2	teaspoons whole-grain Dijon mustard
	Coarse salt and freshly ground black pepper
2	teaspoons chopped fresh dill

- Bring a large pot of salted water to a boil. Add the haricot vert. Cook until al dente, about 3 minutes. Remove with a slotted spoon, and "shock" the haricot vert by transferring them to a bowl of ice water to set the color and stop the cooking. Once chilled, remove to a plate lined with paper towels. Do not leave the haricot vert in the water or the beans may become too waterlogged.

- Heat the oil in a large sauté pan over medium-high heat. Add the beans and mustard. Season with the salt and pepper to taste. Cook, stirring, until heated through, 3 to 5 minutes. Toss with the dill. Taste and adjust for seasoning with salt and pepper and serve immediately.

GREEN BEANS WITH RED ONION

Makes 4 servings

This recipe combines opposite flavors and textures to create an interesting vegetable side dish. Green beans are paired with mustard, vinegar, sugar, and red onions. It's crisp and colorful.

Mustard is related to cabbage and broccoli and produces three main kinds of seeds—black, brown, and yellow. Of these, black seeds are the most pungent. Brown mustard seeds are slightly less spicy. The mildest of the three varieties are the white or yellow seeds. Heating the seeds in the oil is a technique common in Indian cuisine known as *tarka*.

1	plus 1 tablespoons olive oil
1	tablespoon mustard seeds
2	tablespoons white wine vinegar
2	teaspoons sugar
1	small red onion, thinly sliced
¾	pound green beans, trimmed

- Heat 1 tablespoon oil in a large sauté pan over medium heat until hot, but not smoking. Add the mustard seeds and cook, stirring, until they pop and darken slightly, about 2 minutes. Transfer the seeds and oil to a large bowl. Wipe the sauté pan with paper towels and set aside.

- Combine the vinegar and sugar in a medium saucepan over medium heat. Stir until the sugar is dissolved and set aside to cool.

- Heat the remaining 1 tablespoon oil in the reserved sauté pan over medium heat. Add the onion and cook, stirring, until golden brown, about 10 minutes.

- Add the vinegar mixture and the sautéed onions to the mustard oil and stir to combine.

- Bring a large pot of salted water to a boil. Add the green beans. Cook until tender, 5 to 7 minutes. Remove with a slotted spoon and "shock" the green beans by transferring them to a bowl of ice water to set the color and stop the cooking. Once chilled, remove the beans to a plate lined with paper towels and pat dry.

- Add the green beans to the mustard oil and red onion mixture. Toss to combine and coat. Taste and adjust for seasoning with salt and pepper. Serve at room temperature or chilled.

The bandana look catches on with
Atlanta Falcons linebacker Chris Draft.

PECAN-TOASTED GREEN BEANS

Makes 6 servings

"Tipped and tailed" is an expression referring to removing both the stem end and the tip end of the green bean. Most chefs remove the stems but leave the tip end on—it's more attractive.

This recipe is a southern version of Green Beans Amandine, which is made with almonds and was the rage in the '70s.

1½   pounds haicot verts or other thin green beans, stems trimmed
½   cup pecans, chopped
3   tablespoons olive oil
1   tablespoon chopped fresh parsley
    Coarse salt and freshly ground black pepper

- Bring a large pot of salted water to a boil and add the green beans. Cook until tender, 5 to 7 minutes. Remove with a slotted spoon and "shock" the green beans by transferring them to a bowl of ice water to set the color and stop the cooking. Once chilled, remove to a plate lined with paper towels and pat dry.

- Meanwhile, in a medium skillet over medium heat combine the pecans, oil, and parsley. Cook, stirring occasionally, until the pecans are toasted, 3 to 5 minutes.

- Add the beans and toss to coat and combine. Taste and adjust for seasoning with the salt and pepper. Serve immediately.

DROPPIN' KNOWLEDGE

To chop fresh herbs, gather the leaves into a tight ball on the cutting board. Make a bridge, curling your fingers under and tucking your thumb. Slice the herbs, bringing the chef's knife down and backward while sliding the broad side against the bridge of the other hand. Once sliced, then hold the handle firmly in one hand, rest the other palm on top of the blade, and rock the knife back and forth over the herbs to finely chop them.

[SEE PHOTO ON PAGE 82]

GREEN BEANS WITH HOT PEPPER RELISH

Makes 6 servings

This colorful side dish is sweet, spicy, and has a little vinegar kick. Jalepeños are fairly mild. If you really like hot foods, try this relish with a serrano, cayenne, or even a Scotch bonnet pepper.

When shopping for fresh chiles, look for those with smooth, tight skin and a thick, meaty body. They should have some heft relative to their diminutive size. When handling hot peppers, use surgical gloves or dishwashing gloves to protect your hands. Once you've begun working with any hot chiles, be very careful not to touch any part of your body, especially your eyes. After you've finished, wash your knife and cutting board with hot, soapy water.

1½	pounds green beans, stems trimmed
2	tablespoons olive oil
2	shallots, finely chopped
3	red bell peppers, seeded and finely chopped
1	jalepeño chile, seeded and finely chopped
2	garlic cloves, finely chopped
3	tablespoons cider vinegar
1	teaspoon sugar
	Coarse salt and freshly ground black pepper

- Bring a large pot of salted water to a boil and add the green beans. Cook until tender, 5 to 7 minutes. Remove with a slotted spoon and "shock" the green beans by transferring them to a bowl of ice water to set the color and stop the cooking. Once chilled, remove to a plate lined with paper towels and pat dry.

- Meanwhile, heat the oil in a large sauté pan over medium heat until hot but not smoking. Add the shallots and cook until just softened, 2 to 3 minutes. Add the bell peppers and jalepeño and sauté over medium-high heat, stirring until peppers are softened, about 3 minutes. Add the garlic and cook until fragrant, 45 to 60 seconds.

- Add the vinegar and sugar and stir to combine. Cook, stirring occasionally, until the liquid is evaporated, about 2 minutes.

- Add the green beans and toss to combine and coat. Taste and adjust for seasoning with the salt and pepper. Serve immediately.

SPICED GREEN BEANS WITH MINT

Makes 6 servings

When green beans are in season in the summertime, it seems there's no end. Here's another green bean recipe to shake up your side dishes.

Shallots are members of the onion family with a mild, garlic flavor. Used in soups, salads, and sauces the shallot has a brown papery skin as opposed to the whitish skin of the garlic.

1½	pounds green beans, stems trimmed
1	cup vegetable oil
6	medium shallots, thinly sliced crosswise and separated into rings
1	small fresh Thai or serrano chile, thinly sliced crosswise
½	cup chopped fresh mint
	Coarse salt and freshly ground black pepper

- Bring a large pot of salted water to a boil and add the green beans. Cook until tender, 5 to 7 minutes. Remove with a slotted spoon and "shock" the green beans by transferring them to a bowl of ice water to set the color and stop the cooking. Once chilled, remove to a plate lined with paper towels and pat dry.

- Meanwhile in a medium sauté pan over medium heat, add the oil and heat until hot, but not smoking. Working in batches, fry the shallots, turning frequently, until golden brown, about 4 minutes per batch.

- Using a slotted spoon, transfer the shallots to a plate lined with paper towels to drain.

- Remove all but 1 tablespoon oil from the sauté pan. Add the chile and cook over medium heat, stirring, until softened, about 2 minutes.

- Add the beans and toss until heated through, about 2 minutes. Remove from the heat. Add the fried shallots and mint. Toss to coat and combine. Taste and adjust for seasoning with the salt and pepper. Serve immediately.

POLE BEANS WITH BACON

Makes 8 servings

Pole beans are so called because they will grow up a pole as opposed to a bush bean like snap beans. Frankly, they will twirl around all kinds of support—strings, poles, and fences—and they'll climb as high as ten to fifteen feet if you let them. Gardeners with smaller plots love pole beans because they can have a large harvest of beans using very little space.

These beans have a distinct, nutty flavor. When buying pole beans, check for freshness by breaking one in half. It should snap and taste flavorful with a hint of sweetness. Don't buy beans that are dull, wilted, or limp.

2	pounds fresh pole beans, tipped and tailed
3	slices bacon, coarsely chopped
1	cup water
¼	teaspoon sugar
	Coarse salt and freshly ground black pepper

- Cut the beans into 1¼-inch pieces.

- Heat a medium saucepan over medium heat. Add the bacon and cook until the fat is rendered and the bacon is crisp, about 5 minutes. With a slotted spoon, remove the bacon to a plate lined with paper towels to drain.

- Add the water and sugar to the saucepan and bring to a boil. Add the beans and reduce the heat to simmer. Cook the beans until tender, about 15 minutes. Taste and adjust for seasoning with the salt and pepper. Sprinkle with the bacon and serve immediately.

ZUCCHINI COUSCOUS

Makes 4 servings

This recipe is a great way to disguise zucchini when it's coming out of your ears in the garden. Try a mixture of yellow squash and zucchini for a more colorful mix.

Couscous is not a grain as many think, but a type of pasta that is made from durum wheat and water. It is a staple in many North African countries. Over the last decade, it's popped up on American menus and dinner tables. Instant couscous is about as easy as you can get—add to boiling water, cover, remove from the heat, and let it rehydrate.

3	zucchini
2	tablespoons olive oil
½	teaspoon ground cumin
½	teaspoon paprika
	Coarse salt and freshly ground black pepper
1	cup boiling water
⅔	cup couscous

- Cut the zucchini into ¼-inch dice. Heat the oil in a large sauté pan over medium heat until very hot, but not smoking. Add the zucchini and season with the cumin, paprika, and salt and pepper to taste. Cook, stirring, until just tender, 3 to 5 minutes.

- Add the water and bring to a boil. Add the couscous and stir to combine. Remove from the heat. Cover and let stand until the water is absorbed, about 5 minutes. Fluff the couscous with a fork. Taste and adjust for seasoning with salt and pepper. Serve immediately.

ASPARAGUS WITH TOASTED ALMONDS

Makes 4 servings

To trim asparagus, cut off the last inch or two of the stem, or wherever it snaps naturally when you bend it near the end. Large asparagus is more mature, less tender, and may also need to be peeled.

This asparagus recipe will be a simple and elegant addition to your recipe box. As the stock reduces, the natural sugars in the asparagus create a light glaze. Serve this with grilled rib-eye steaks or the Mustard and Herb-Crusted Roast Pork (page 139) and a side of rice for a good supper. To toast the almonds, heat a medium dry skillet over medium heat. Toast the almonds, stirring frequently until golden brown and fragrant, about five minutes.

1	pound asparagus, trimmed
½	cup homemade chicken stock or reduced-fat, low-sodium chicken broth or water
2	tablespoons unsalted butter
	Coarse salt and freshly ground black pepper
	Pinch of sugar
3	tablespoons sliced almonds, toasted
1	tablespoon fresh lemon juice

- Cut the asparagus diagonally into ½-inch pieces.
- Bring the stock and butter to a boil in a medium sauté pan over medium heat. Season with the salt and pepper.
- Add the asparagus and sugar. Simmer, uncovered, until the asparagus is crisp-tender and the liquid is reduced to a glaze, about 3 minutes. Add the almonds and lemon juice. Taste and adjust for seasoning with salt and pepper. Serve immediately.

CAULIFLOWER-LEEK PURÉE

Makes 4 servings

Cauliflower is sort of the forgotten vegetable. It is a member of the cabbage family and is composed of bunches of tiny, creamy white florets on stalks of the same color. The entire white portion—called the curd—is edible.

Whole-milk yogurt will produce a smoother and creamier purée than nonfat or low-fat yogurt. If you want to really splurge, skip the yogurt and use heavy cream instead.

1   head cauliflower, separated into florets
1   leek, white part with 1 inch of green, well washed, cut into ½-inch slices
¼   cup plain yogurt
⅛   teaspoon freshly grated nutmeg
        Coarse salt and freshly ground black pepper

- Bring a large pot of salted water to a boil. Add the cauliflower and leek and cook until very tender, about 15 minutes. Drain well in a colander, and then return the vegetables to the pot and toss over high heat to remove any excess moisture.

- Place half the vegetables in a food processor with half the yogurt. Process until smooth. Repeat with the remaining vegetables and yogurt. Add the nutmeg and season to taste with the salt and pepper. Serve immediately.

GARLIC KALE

Makes 4 to 6 servings

Kale is a winter green. It's a member of the cabbage family closely related to collard greens. Both crinkly and smooth varieties are an excellent source of vitamin A. There are many varieties and colors—usually dark green with shades of blue and purple.

This recipe uses a technique called chiffonade. To chiffonade is to slice an herb or leafy vegetable into very thin strands. To do this, stack the leaves one on top of the other and roll tightly into a cylinder. Slice the cylinder of leaves crosswise into thin strips.

3   medium garlic cloves, chopped

1   teaspoon coarse salt

2   tablespoons olive oil

2   medium bunches kale, tough stems removed and discarded, leaves very thinly sliced

      Freshly ground black pepper

- Mash together the garlic and 1 teaspoon salt to form a coarse paste.
- Heat the oil in a medium skillet over medium-high heat. Add the garlic-salt mixture and the kale. Season with the pepper to taste. Cook until the kale is bright green and slightly wilted, about 4 minutes. Taste and adjust for seasoning with coarse salt and pepper. Serve immediately.

DROPPIN' KNOWLEDGE

To make garlic paste, place a peeled garlic clove on a clean work surface. Smash the clove with the broad side of a chef's knife. Sprinkle kosher salt over the garlic and then chop. The grains of salt act as "little knives" helping to crush the garlic. To achieve an even smoother paste, after crushing the garlic rub the broad side of the knife over the garlic and salt firmly pressing on the cutting board.

[SEE PHOTO ON PAGE 82]

KALE WITH BACON

Makes 8 servings

Hearty winter greens like kale often grow in sandy soil. To clean the greens fill the sink with cold water and add the greens. Swish well and the soil will sink to the bottom. Lift the greens from the water and remove the greens from the sink. Drain the water and sediment. Clean the sink and repeat, swishing greens more vigorously during the second rinse. Repeat the process until the water is clean. Occasionally very dirty leaves will need to be rinsed individually. Many times recipes will call for the leaves to have water clinging to them, so do not dry the leaves unless specified in the recipe.

Greens are hands-down a nutritional powerhouse. They are extremely low in calories and they provide substantial amounts of vitamins A and C—good and good for you.

8	slices bacon
2	shallots, chopped
3	garlic cloves, chopped
2	bunches kale, stems cut away, leaves torn into 1-inch pieces
2	cups vegetable or homemade chicken stock or reduced-fat, low-sodium chicken broth
	Coarse salt and freshly ground black pepper

- In a large sauté pan over medium heat cook the bacon until crisp. Transfer to a plate lined with paper towels, drain, and crumble.

- Remove and discard all but 2 tablespoons bacon drippings from the pan. Add the shallots and garlic, and sauté over medium heat until tender, about 2 minutes. Add the kale and stock. Cover and cook, stirring occasionally, until the kale is wilted and slightly tender, about 10 minutes. Uncover and continue cooking, stirring occasionally, until completely tender, about 10 minutes.

- Taste and adjust for seasoning with the salt and pepper. Transfer the kale to a serving bowl and sprinkle with the bacon. Serve immediately.

SAUTÉED SWISS CHARD

Makes 6 to 8 servings

Some cooks won't venture farther than spinach when considering greens, but there are plenty to choose from: Swiss chard, kale, beet, turnip, and collard greens, which thrive in winter. Today's market even has more exotic choices to try such as arugula, escarole, red mustard, or mizuna. Give them a try.

Swiss chard comes with both red and green stems. It tastes similar to beet greens and can be used interchangeably with spinach or beet greens in most recipes. The red variety is usually a bit more tender. To avoid waste and obtain as much fiber as possible, separate the leaves and stems and cook the tougher stems first.

3	pounds Swiss chard (preferably red), about 4 bunches, washed
¼	cup olive oil
3	garlic cloves, finely chopped
½	cup water
	Coarse salt and freshly ground black pepper

- Cut the stems and center ribs from the chard leaves. Thinly slice the stems and center ribs and chop the leaves.

- In a large, heavy-bottom sauté pan, heat the oil over medium-high heat. Cook the stems and ribs, stirring, until crisp-tender, 3 to 4 minutes. Add the garlic and cook, stirring, just until fragrant, 45 to 60 seconds. Add the leaves and cook, stirring, until wilted. Reduce the heat to medium. Add the water and season with the salt and pepper to taste. Cover and cook until the leaves are tender, about 4 minutes. Taste and adjust for seasoning with salt and pepper. Serve immediately.

SAUTÉED SPINACH WITH GARLIC

Makes 4 servings

This is a very easy recipe to toss together. You can use frozen spinach in a pinch just make sure it is well-drained. Frozen spinach is a handy vegetable to keep in the freezer. It can be defrosted and sautéed in a simple recipe such as this or used in more complex dishes.

Be very careful when toasting the garlic in oil. If it burns it will taste acrid and bitter. Basically, you will just need to start over if the garlic burns.

2	tablespoons olive oil
2	tablespoons unsalted butter
6	garlic cloves, finely chopped
4	(5-ounce) bags baby spinach
	Coarse salt and freshly ground black pepper
2	tablespoons freshly grated Parmigiano-Reggiano cheese

- Heat the olive oil and butter in a large skillet over medium-high heat. Add the garlic and cook until fragrant and lightly golden, 45 to 60 seconds.
- Add the spinach and toss to coat. Sauté until just wilted, 2 to 3 minutes. Remove from the heat. Season to taste with the salt and pepper and sprinkle the Parmigiano-Reggiano cheese on top. Serve immediately.

Makes 4 servings

Spinach is a standard green used frequently in recipes and available year-round. It's great raw or cooked and may be substituted for many other greens, especially where color is important. Spinach cooks far more quickly than tougher greens like kale, chard, and collards, so adjust the cooking time accordingly.

This recipe is slightly sweet with golden raisins. Try sprinkling it with lightly toasted pine nuts, pecans, or almonds for a little crunch.

½	cup golden raisins
½	cup boiling water, wine, or homemade chicken stock or reduced-fat, low-sodium chicken broth
2	tablespoons olive oil
2	shallots, chopped
4	(5-ounce) bags baby spinach
	Coarse salt and freshly ground black pepper

- Place the raisins in a small bowl. Pour the water, wine, or chicken stock over the raisins. Let rest to plump and rehydrate for 10 to 15 minutes.
- Heat the olive oil in a large pan over medium-low heat. Add the shallots and cook until translucent, 3 to 5 minutes. Add the spinach and cook until wilted. Drain the golden raisins, discarding the liquid, and add them to the spinach. Stir to combine. Taste and adjust for seasoning with the salt and pepper. Serve immediately.

CREAMED SPINACH WITH GARLIC

Makes 6 servings

This dish is rich and comforting. This simple method avoids making a béchamel sauce and is a simple cream reduction.

Béchamel sauce is a French white sauce made with milk and a roux of butter and flour. For creamed spinach, the proportions are one tablespoon each of flour and butter to one cup of milk. (It's a great way to cut fat and calories—low-fat milk works as well as whole milk.) Then proceed by adding the wilted spinach, garlic, nutmeg, salt, and pepper.

1	cup water
2½	pounds baby spinach
1½	cups heavy cream
4	garlic cloves, very finely chopped
	Freshly grated nutmeg
	Coarse salt and freshly ground black pepper

- Using a 2-quart heavy saucepan over high heat, bring the water to a boil. Add the spinach and toss, cooking until wilted, 2 to 3 minutes. Transfer the spinach to a colander or sieve. Remove the excess liquid by pressing on the spinach with the back of a wooden spoon.

- Combine the cream, garlic, nutmeg, and salt and pepper to taste in a saucepan over high heat. Bring to a boil, reduce to medium-high heat, and continue cooking until reduced by half.

- Add the spinach to the cream mixture, and toss until coated and heated through. Taste and adjust for seasoning with salt and pepper. Serve immediately.

COLLARD GREENS WITH RED ONION

Makes 8 servings

Southerners love their greens. In the South, a large quantity of greens to serve a family is commonly referred to as a "mess." The exact quantity that constitutes a "mess" varies from family to family. Typically, greens are served with corn bread to dip into the potlikker. Potlikker is the highly concentrated, vitamin-filled broth that results from the long, slow cooking of the greens.

The traditional way to cook greens is to boil or simmer them slowly with a piece of salt pork or ham hock for a long time (this tempers their tough texture and smooth out their bitter flavor) until they are very soft. Here we're using just a little bacon for flavor, but not too much fat.

2	slices bacon, chopped
2	medium red onions, coarsely chopped (about 2 cups)
1¼	cups homemade chicken stock or reduced-fat, low-sodium chicken broth
¼	cup cider vinegar
2	tablespoons firmly packed dark brown sugar
½	teaspoon red pepper flakes
4	pounds collard greens, preferably small leaves, coarse stems and ribs discarded
	Coarse salt and freshly ground black pepper

- In a large, heavy-bottom pot cook the bacon over medium heat until crisp. Transfer to a plate lined with paper towels, and drain.

- Sauté the onions in the bacon drippings, stirring occasionally, until browned slightly and softened, 3 to 5 minutes. Add the stock, vinegar, brown sugar, red pepper flakes, and bacon, stirring until the sugar is dissolved.

- Wash, drain, and chop the leaves and thin stems of the greens. Add about half to the pot, tossing until slightly wilted. Add the remaining collards and toss to combine. Reduce the heat to medium low, cover, and simmer the collards until tender, about 30 minutes. Taste and adjust for seasoning with the salt and pepper. Serve immediately.

Marvin and friend Johnny Rivers, executive chef
of the Isaac Hayes' restaurant in Memphis.

ACORN SQUASH
WITH PECANS & GOAT CHEESE

Makes 4 servings

Acorn squash are oval winter squash with a ribbed, dark green skin and slightly sweet orange flesh. They are very easy to prepare and excellent if simply baked and topped with butter, brown sugar, maple syrup, or honey and a pinch of nutmeg and cinnamon.

This recipe combines the squash with pecans, thyme, and goat cheese. The goat cheese melts in the oven and makes a creamy, almost sauce-like filling. The slightly tangy cheese marries nicely with the earthy taste of the squash.

2	acorn squash, halved crosswise and seeded
	Coarse salt
3	tablespoons unsalted butter, melted
2/3	cup chopped pecans
2	tablespoons maple syrup, plus more to drizzle
2	sprigs fresh thyme, chopped
4	ounces goat cheese
	Coarse salt and freshly ground black pepper

- Preheat the oven to 375°F. Sprinkle the inside of the squash with salt and brush with butter. Turn the squash upside down on a baking sheet, and bake until tender, about 30 minutes.

- Using a small bowl combine the pecans, maple syrup, and thyme. Turn the squash upright on the baking sheet. Fill the hollow of each squash with the pecan mixture, reserving about 3 tablespoons.

- Slice the goat cheese crosswise into four equal rounds. Place a round of cheese on top of each pecan mixture. Sprinkle with the reserved pecans. Season to taste with the salt and pepper. Bake 10 minutes more. Drizzle with additional syrup if desired. Serve immediately.

SPICED CARROTS

Makes 6 servings

This dish is crunchy, colorful, and delicious. Carrots will keep in the refrigerator in a plastic bag up to ten days. Remove the green tops before storing, since they will shorten the carrots' shelf life.

Paprika is dried, ground, sweet red pepper. It is mildly flavored and prized in the kitchen for its brilliant red color. Make sure to keep paprika and other ground spices no longer than three to six months.

¼	teaspoon ground cumin
¼	teaspoon paprika
	Pinch of cayenne (or to taste)
2	teaspoons olive oil
1	tablespoon honey
	Coarse salt and freshly ground black pepper
1½	pounds carrots, cut into julienne or matchsticks
1	teaspoon white wine vinegar
1½	tablespoons chopped, fresh flat-leaf parsley

- Using a small, nonstick sauté pan over low heat, combine the cumin, paprika, cayenne, and oil. Cook, stirring, until fragrant, about 2 minutes. Remove from the heat and cool slightly. Add the honey and season with the salt and pepper to taste.

- Using a 4-quart saucepan, cook the carrots in boiling salted water until tender, 2 to 3 minutes. Transfer to a colander and drain thoroughly.

- Place the warm carrots in a medium bowl. Add the spiced oil, vinegar, and parsley. Toss to coat and combine. Taste and adjust for seasoning with salt and pepper. Serve immediately.

BUTTERNUT SQUASH
WITH CUMIN & CORIANDER

Makes 6 servings

Warm spices give this squash dish a nice kick, especially the freshly ground black pepper. Green, black, and white peppercorns are small dried berries from a tropical vine. (Pink peppercorns aren't actually peppercorns at all, but the dried berry of a rose plant.) Green peppercorns are harvested when under-ripe. They are usually packed in brine. They have a mild flavor and soft consistency and texture. Black peppercorns are harvested while they are still green, allowed to ferment, and sun dried until they turn brownish black. They have a hot, piney taste. White peppercorns are simply the result of removing the black outer coating. White pepper is milder in flavor.

1	tablespoon cumin seeds
2	teaspoons whole black peppercorns
1	teaspoon coriander seeds
2	teaspoons sugar
4	pounds butternut squash, peeled, seeded, cut into 1-inch cubes
1/3	cup olive oil
	Coarse salt and freshly ground black pepper

- Preheat the oven to 400°F. Using a medium sauté pan over medium heat, combine the cumin, peppercorns, and coriander seeds. Toast the seeds, stirring, until fragrant, about 5 minutes. Cool slightly. Place the toasted seeds in an electric spice grinder and process until fine. Transfer to a large bowl. Add the sugar and stir to combine.

- Add the cubed squash and oil, and season to taste with the salt and pepper. Toss to coat. Transfer the squash to a rimmed baking sheet. Bake until tender and lightly brown, stirring occasionally, about 45 minutes. Taste and adjust for seasoning with salt and pepper. Serve immediately.

DROPPIN' KNOWLEDGE

It's important that your cutting board does not move or wiggle while you chop or you might cut yourself. To prevent this, place a damp paper towel or a piece of non-slip rubber mesh that is often used under area rugs underneath your board.

GRITS, RICE & POTATOES

No-carb potatoes!

I thought that might grab you. Ok, now that I have your full attention, think about this. Carbs, like protein, serve a purpose, so I suggest that you choose your food groups in moderation. If you're a busy person like most adults with careers and families, it is far too difficult to maintain strict dietary conditions that cancel out entire food categories, especially over time. Unless you have health concerns, you should occasionally feed that craving for shrimp and grits, or floral rice, or fried chicken and mashed potatoes. One helping (not two), the appropriate size for one adult (not three) should be enjoyed without guilt. Simply put, keep everything in moderation and you will be just fine.

JALEPEÑO CHEESE GRITS CASSEROLE

Makes 8 servings

This simple casserole is a familiar dish in the South. Perfect for potlucks, brunches, or weddings—Cheese Grits Casserole is a standard. Use this recipe as a guide and make it your own. Add more chiles to give it some real heat, add chopped scallions or herbs, or switch up the cheeses and try adding freshly grated Parmigiano-Reggiano or Gruyère.

Cheddar, sometimes called "rat cheese" in the South, is traditionally used in this dish. Cheddar's flavor ranges from mild, nutty, and creamy to extra sharp, rich, and robust. If you want a little tang, try white Cheddar.

4	cups water
1	teaspoon salt
1	cup coarse-ground grits
1½	cups shredded sharp Cheddar cheese
½	cup low-fat milk
2	tablespoons unsalted butter
	Coarse salt and freshly ground black pepper
4	large eggs, lightly beaten
¼	teaspoon cayenne (or to taste)
1	jalapeño chile, seeded and finely chopped

- Preheat the oven to 350°F. Lightly grease a casserole.

- Bring the water and salt to a boil in a large saucepan. Stir in the grits and return to a boil. Reduce the heat to simmer and cook until thick, about 20 minutes. Remove from the heat. Add the cheese, milk, and butter. Season with the salt and pepper to taste and stir to combine. Add the eggs and stir until well incorporated. Add the cayenne and jalapeño.

- Spoon the mixture into the prepared casserole. Bake until golden brown, about 1 hour. Remove to a rack to cool slightly before serving.

CHEDDAR GRITS SOUFFLÉ

Makes 8 servings

Southerners have a tendency to call anything baked with beaten egg whites a soufflé. This is not a true soufflé, but it will rise in the oven similar to a soufflé. The name itself originates from the French *souffler*, which means "to blow up." Beating egg whites is quite simply incorporating air into the egg-white foam. Properly beaten egg whites are the key to the rising of this dish. While the dish is in the oven, the air trapped inside the egg whites expands, causing the dish to rise.

To prevent the soufflé from sticking, coat the dish with room-temperature butter, and then place it in the refrigerator. As the butter chills and firms you can very clearly see any spots you might have missed.

2	cups homemade chicken stock or reduced-fat, low-sodium chicken broth, plus 1 cup water (or use 3 cups water)
½	cup milk
½	cup heavy cream
2	teaspoons salt
1	cup coarse-ground grits
5	large eggs, separated
1½	cups grated sharp Cheddar cheese
2	garlic cloves, finely chopped
½	cup (1 stick) unsalted butter, plus more for the dish
	Coarse salt and freshly ground black pepper
½	teaspoon hot sauce (or to taste)
2	scallions, thinly sliced

CHEDDAR GRITS SOUFFLÉ

(continued)

- Butter a 2-quart casserole or soufflé dish. Using a large, heavy-bottom saucepan over high heat, bring the stock, water, milk, cream, and salt to a boil. Gradually stir in the grits. Reduce the heat to medium and cook, stirring often, until the grits are thick and creamy, about 20 minutes.

- Using a large bowl whisk the egg yolks, and temper them by whisking in a spoonful of the hot grits. Stir the yolks into remaining grits. Add the cheese, garlic, and butter. Season to taste with the salt, black pepper, and hot sauce. Set aside to cool to room temperature.

- An hour before serving, preheat the oven to 375°F. In the bowl of a heavy-duty mixer fitted with the whisk attachment, whisk the egg whites with a pinch of salt on medium speed until foamy. Increase the speed to high and whip until stiff peaks form, 2 to 3 minutes.

- Add about one-quarter of the beaten egg whites to the grits mixture and stir until well mixed. Pour this mixture and the scallions over the remaining whites and fold them together as lightly as possible.

- Pour the mixture into the prepared dish. Bake until the grits are set, 30 to 40 minutes. (If the surface begins to overbrown, cover with foil.) Serve immediately.

SHRIMP & GRITS CASSEROLE

Makes 6 servings

Every restaurant across the low country has its own version of shrimp and grits. It's a Charleston and Savannah classic. But grits aren't just for breakfast—or southerners—anymore. Breakfast, brunch, lunch, or dinner—this dish will always satisfy.

Old Bay is a combination of celery salt, ground mustard, red pepper, black pepper, bay leaves, cloves, allspice, ginger, mace, cardamom, cinnamon, and paprika. It's highly flavored to enhance the sweet taste of the shrimp. Cook the shrimp in their shells for the best flavor and texture, and make sure not to overcook them.

5	cups plus 1½ cups water
1	tablespoon Old Bay seasoning
1½	pounds unpeeled, medium fresh shrimp
	Vegetable oil for the baking dish
1½	plus ½ cups milk
½	teaspoon salt
1	cup coarse-ground grits
2	large eggs, lightly beaten
2	garlic cloves, very finely chopped
1½	cups shredded Cheddar cheese
¼	teaspoon paprika
1	tablespoon chopped fresh parsley

- Bring 5 cups of the water and the Old Bay seasoning to boil in a large stockpot. Add the shrimp. Cook just until the shrimp turn pink, 2 to 3 minutes. Peel and devein the shrimp.

- Preheat the oven to 350°F. Lightly grease a 7 x 11-inch baking dish. Using a medium saucepan over high heat, bring the remaining 1½ cups water, 1½ cups milk, and salt to a boil. Stir in the grits. Reduce the heat, cover, and simmer for 10 minutes. Remove from the heat.

- Combine the eggs and remaining ½ cup milk in a large bowl. Gradually add the cooked grits, stirring constantly. Add the peeled shrimp, garlic, and 1 cup Cheddar cheese. Transfer to prepared baking dish. Sprinkle with the remaining ½ cup cheese. Bake until browned and bubbly, about 30 minutes. Remove to a rack to cool slightly. Sprinkle with paprika and parsley. Serve immediately.

GRITS WITH FONTINA & BACON

Makes 6 servings

Grits are made from corn. Corn kernels are soaked in lye and the casing is removed to make hominy. The lye is rinsed out very well and the corn is left to harden. Then the swollen hominy is ground up to the texture of tiny pellets. These pellets are known as grits in the South and polenta in Italy.

This recipe has an Italian feel with the addition of the Italian cheeses. Fontina is a full-fat, semi-hard cheese with a distinctive, sweet taste. Made from whole cow's milk, the rind is thin and close-textured, while the interior is rather soft and elastic and varies in color from whitish-yellow to yellow. Try a mild Cheddar or Gouda as a substitute.

5	slices bacon
1	Vidalia onion, chopped
1	garlic clove, finely chopped
5	cups homemade chicken stock or reduced-fat, low-sodium chicken broth
1	cup fresh corn kernels, about 2 ears
1	cup coarse-ground grits
3	ounces Fontina cheese, grated
½	cup freshly grated Parmigiano-Reggiano cheese
2	tablespoons chopped fresh parsley
	Coarse salt and freshly ground black pepper

- Using a large, heavy-bottom sauté pan over medium-high heat, cook the bacon until crisp, about 8 minutes. Transfer the bacon to a plate lined with paper towels to drain. Pour off all but 2 tablespoons of the drippings.

- Add the onion and garlic and sauté until golden brown, about 2 minutes. Add the chicken broth, corn, and bacon. Bring to a boil. Gradually add the grits, whisking constantly. Cook until the grits are soft and thick, stirring frequently, about 20 minutes. Add the cheeses, stirring until melted, about 2 minutes. Add the parsley and stir to combine. Taste and adjust for seasoning with salt and pepper. Serve immediately.

[SEE PHOTO ON PAGE 114]

SPICY SHRIMP WITH SAUSAGE ON GRITS

Makes 4 servings

Louisiana-style andouille is a smoked sausage that's wonderful and full of flavor. Andouille is made with coarsely ground pork butt, shank, and a small amount of pork fat. It is highly seasoned with salt, cracked black pepper, and garlic. The andouille is then slowly smoked over pecan wood and sugarcane. When smoked, it becomes very dark to almost black in color. Andouille is available online and in some specialty stores.

Green hot pepper sauce is made from jalapeño peppers and is a little milder than hot sauce made with red peppers. If you want to give this dish a little more heat, feel free to use traditional red hot sauce.

FOR THE CREAM SAUCE:

⅓	cup green hot sauce
¼	cup dry white wine
1	shallot, chopped
1	tablespoon fresh lemon juice
½	cup whipping cream

FOR THE GRITS:

2	tablespoons vegetable oil
1	Vidalia onion, grated
1	cup fresh corn kernels, about 2 ears
2	cups milk
2	cups water
2	cups coarse-ground grits
2	tablespoons unsalted butter
	Coarse salt and freshly ground black pepper

(continued)

FOR THE SHRIMP AND SAUSAGE:

1/4	cup olive oil
8	ounces smoked andouille sausage
1	red bell pepper, seeded and chopped
1	yellow bell pepper, seeded and chopped
1	Vidalia onion, chopped
4	garlic cloves, chopped
20	uncooked large shrimp, peeled and deveined
4	plum tomatoes, chopped
1	teaspoon Cajun seasoning
1	teaspoon Old Bay seasoning
	Coarse salt and freshly ground black pepper

- For the cream sauce, combine the hot sauce, wine, shallot, and lemon juice in a heavy, medium saucepan. Boil over medium heat until reduced to 1/2 cup, about 15 minutes. Stir in the whipping cream.

- For the grits, in a medium saucepan heat the vegetable oil over medium heat. Add the onion and cook, stirring, until transparent, about 2 minutes. Add the corn and cook, stirring occasionally, or until the kernels become soft, about 5 minutes. Add the milk and water and bring the mixture to a boil. Whisk in the grits. Reduce the heat to low and simmer, stirring constantly, until the grits are thick, 30 to 45 minutes. Stir in the butter and salt and pepper to taste.

- Meanwhile, for the shrimp and sausage, heat the olive oil in a heavy, medium skillet over medium heat. Add the sausage, bell peppers, onion, and garlic. Sauté until the vegetables are tender, about 8 minutes. Add the shrimp, tomatoes, Cajun seasoning, and Old Bay seasoning. Sauté until the shrimp are opaque in the center, about 6 minutes. Season to taste with the salt and pepper.

- Bring the cream sauce to a simmer. Divide the grits equally among four plates. Spoon the shrimp mixture over the grits. Drizzle the cream sauce over all and serve.

DROPPIN' KNOWLEDGE

In a restaurant, hot food is always served on warm plates. This helps the food stay warm longer. You can do this at home by warming your plates in the oven. Adjust your oven racks to the bottom and center positions. Preheat the oven to 150°F to 200°F. Line a baking sheet with a kitchen towel and stack the plates on the prepared baking sheet. Check the plates after 8 to 10 minutes. They should be warm to the touch but not too hot to hold.

*Marvin grillin' and chillin' at Memphis in May with producer
and coauthor Virginia Willis and kitchen manager Judy Sellner.*

WILD RICE PANCAKES

Makes about 12

Wild rice is actually not true rice, but annual aquatic grass that produces an edible seed. It grows in the shallows of lakes and rivers throughout eastern and north central United States and southern Canada.

Native to North America, wild rice has been harvested and eaten by Native Americans for centuries. It's prized for its distinctive natural flavor, texture, and unique, almost nutty flavor. The gray-brown grain is about twice the length of ordinary rice grains. Wild rice goes well with rich meat and game dishes like venison and duck.

1	cup wild rice	½	teaspoon chopped fresh thyme
2⅔	cups water		Coarse salt and freshly ground black pepper
1	teaspoon coarse salt		
3	tablespoons unsalted butter	½	cup pecans, toasted and chopped
½	cup finely diced carrot		
½	cup finely diced celery	2	large eggs, lightly beaten
1	cup finely chopped onion	¾	cup milk
1	scallion, finely chopped	1	cup all-purpose flour

- In a heavy saucepan combine the rice, water, and salt and simmer the mixture, covered, for 45 to 50 minutes, or until the rice is tender and all the water is absorbed. Transfer the rice to a large bowl and let it cool.

- Heat the butter in a heavy skillet over moderate heat. Add the carrot, celery, onion, scallion, and thyme. Season to taste with the salt and pepper. Cook until the onion is translucent, stirring occasionally, 5 to 7 minutes. Add the vegetables to the rice and stir to combine. Add the pecans and stir to combine.

- In a small bowl whisk together the eggs and milk, stir the egg mixture into the rice mixture, and stir in the flour and more salt and pepper to taste.

- Heat the griddle over moderately high heat until it is hot enough so that drops of water scatter over its surface and brush it with vegetable oil. Working in batches, scoop the batter onto the griddle by ¼-cup measures, flatten the pancakes slightly, and cook them for 2 to 3 minutes on each side, or until they are golden. Serve immediately.

BASMATI RICE

Makes 8 servings

Basmati rice is authentic Indian, long-grained, white rice, which has a unique, fragrant, nutty flavor. When cooking rice, the shorter the grain the higher the starch content. So, long-grain rice is lower in starch and will produce cooked rice with separate grains, not creamy and thick like risotto or sushi rice. Texmati is an aromatic rice that's a cross between American long-grain rice and basmati and may be substituted.

This dish has an Indian or eastern flavor with the addition of raisins, cinnamon, and mustard seeds. Serve this flavorful rice dish with roast pork or turkey.

3	cups water
1½	cups basmati rice
¼	cup golden raisins
1	cinnamon stick
1	teaspoon mustard seeds
1	teaspoon coarse salt, plus more for seasoning
2	tablespoons chives, chopped
	Freshly ground black pepper

- In a 3-quart heavy saucepan combine the water, rice, raisins, cinnamon stick, mustard seeds, and salt. Bring to a boil, reduce heat to low, stir, and cover. Cook the rice until the liquid is absorbed, about 20 minutes. Remove from the heat and let rest without removing the cover for 5 minutes. Fluff the rice with a fork. Add the chives, taste, and adjust for seasoning with salt and pepper. Serve immediately.

SAVANNAH RED RICE

Makes 8 servings

Red rice is a low-country favorite. But rice can be temperamental. It can be a pot of hard pellets or dissolve to an unpleasant, gummy mess. The pilaf method is great for cooking long-grain white rice. The rice is first sautéed in oil or butter before covering with water.

In this recipe we use the rendered bacon grease. The water is then brought to a boil before the pan is covered and the heat reduced to cook the rice. It is then removed from the heat and left to rest before serving. With this method, the rice cooks up in separate grains, and sautéing the rice adds a rich layer of flavor.

4	slices bacon, chopped
1	small red bell pepper, seeded and diced
1	small green bell pepper, seeded and diced
1	celery stalk, diced
1	medium onion, diced
2	garlic cloves, finely chopped
2	cups long-grain white rice
2	cups crushed canned tomatoes
2	tablespoons tomato paste
1½	cups water
2	teaspoons hot sauce
	Coarse salt and freshly ground black pepper

- Using a large, heavy-bottom saucepan, cook the bacon over medium-high heat until crisp. Add the red and green bell peppers, celery, onion, and garlic. Cook, stirring, 3 to 4 minutes. Add the rice and stir to coat. Add the tomatoes, tomato paste, water, and hot sauce. Season with the salt and pepper to taste.

- Bring the mixture to a boil and cover. Reduce the heat to simmer and cook until the rice is tender and the liquid is absorbed, 20 to 25 minutes. Remove from the heat and let rest without removing the cover for 5 minutes. Fluff the rice with a fork. Taste and adjust for seasoning with salt and pepper. Serve immediately.

RED PEPPER RICE

Makes 4 servings

Some recipes call for soaking rice before cooking. But soaking rice can make the rice soggy and the grains split. Rinsing rice, however, is a good technique. Rinsing washes away the starch and doesn't cause the problems associated with soaking.

This rice is colorful and zesty. Try it with roast chicken or the Honey and Dijon Mustard Salmon (page 191).

1	tablespoon olive oil
1	medium onion, finely chopped
2	garlic cloves, finely chopped
1	teaspoon paprika
½	teaspoon red pepper flakes
1	large red bell pepper, seeded and finely diced
1	cup long-grain rice
2	cups water
½	teaspoon grated lemon zest
2	sprigs fresh thyme
	Coarse salt and freshly ground black pepper
1	tablespoon fresh lemon juice

- Heat the oil in a saucepan over medium heat. Add the onion and cook, stirring frequently, until the onion has softened, 5 to 7 minutes. Add the garlic, paprika, and red pepper flakes. Cook until fragrant, 45 to 60 seconds.

- Add the bell pepper and cook, stirring frequently, until the pepper is tender, about 5 minutes.

- Add the rice and stir to coat. Add the water, lemon zest, thyme, and salt and pepper to taste. Bring to a boil and then reduce the heat to simmer. Cover and simmer until the rice is cooked through, about 20 minutes. Remove from the heat and let rest without removing the cover for 5 minutes. Fluff rice with a fork. Taste and adjust for seasoning with the salt and pepper. Stir in the lemon juice and serve immediately.

HERB ROASTED POTATOES

Makes 4 servings

It's important to bake these potatoes in a single layer on a heavy-duty baking sheet. The type of bakeware you use can determine the success or failure of a recipe. But getting the most expensive bakeware doesn't guarantee the best results. Double-thick, aluminum, half-sheet pans with rolled edges are standard in restaurant kitchens. These pans cost about fifteen dollars and are ideal for everything from baking cookies, pastries, and breads to roasting meats and vegetables.

Fennel seeds are oval and pale greenish-brown, and very similar in appearance to cumin seeds. They have a very sweet, mild, licorice taste and are perhaps most familiar in Italian sausage. They make a huge difference in plain old roasted potatoes.

¼	cup olive oil, plus more for the baking sheets
2	tablespoons balsamic vinegar
4	sprigs fresh thyme
2	sprigs fresh rosemary
½	teaspoon fennel seeds
5	garlic cloves, peeled
1½	pounds medium red potatoes, cut into 8 wedges
1½	pounds medium Yukon Gold potatoes, cut into 8 wedges
	Coarse salt and freshly ground black pepper

- Preheat the oven to 400°F. Oil a large baking sheet. In a large bowl whisk together the olive oil, vinegar, thyme, rosemary, and fennel to blend. Add the garlic and potatoes and season generously with the salt and pepper. Toss to coat. Using a slotted spoon, transfer the potatoes to the prepared baking sheet, spreading the potatoes in a single layer. Reserve the oil mixture in a bowl.

- Roast the potatoes until golden brown and fork-tender, stirring occasionally, about 1 hour. Transfer them to a serving bowl. Drizzle with the reserved oil and taste and adjust for seasoning with salt and pepper. Toss to coat and combine. Serve immediately.

MIXED MASH

Makes 4 servings

Call it mash, smash, or purée, there's no better side dish for roast beef with flavorful jus or pork chops and gravy. This recipe uses potatoes as the lead, but adds cauliflower and carrot to mix things up.

Select potatoes that are smooth and firm, and without cracks, bruises, or soft spots. Also avoid potatoes with green-tinted skin; they can have a bitter taste. Unlike green vegetables, it's best to start potatoes in cold water and bring the water to a boil. The potatoes cook more evenly and the outside is not over-cooked by the time the inside is cooked.

$2\frac{1}{2}$	pounds Yukon Gold potatoes, peeled and quartered
$1\frac{1}{2}$	cups cauliflower florets
2	garlic cloves, chopped
1	medium carrot, chopped
$\frac{1}{4}$	cup milk
2	tablespoons unsalted butter
	Coarse salt and freshly ground black pepper
1	tablespoon chopped fresh parsley

- Place the potatoes in a large pot of cold, salted water. Bring to a boil. Reduce the heat to simmer and add the cauliflower, garlic, and carrot. Cook until the vegetables are tender but firm, 15 to 20 minutes. Drain and return to the pot. Cook the vegetables in the dry pan, stirring constantly, to remove the excess water, 45 to 60 seconds.

- Add the milk and butter. Using a potato masher, mash until smooth. Taste and adjust for seasoning with salt and pepper. Sprinkle with the parsley and serve immediately.

OVEN FRIES

Makes 4 servings

Russet potatoes, also known as Idaho or russet Burbank potatoes, have a high starch content, so there's more potato and less water. This makes a great oven fry that's crisp and not soggy.

It's very important to preheat the baking sheets before cooking the potatoes. Heating the baking sheets "sears" the potatoes. It seems redundant, but spraying the preheated sheets with nonstick spray will prevent the oiled potatoes from sticking. Finally, make sure to bake them in one layer or they will not crisp properly.

2   **medium russet potatoes**
2   **tablespoons olive oil**
    Coarse salt and freshly ground black pepper

- Preheat the oven to 450°F. Place two heavy-duty baking sheets in the oven to heat at least 15 minutes. Scrub and rinse the potatoes well, and then cut them lengthwise into $\frac{1}{2}$-inch-wide sticks. Place the potato sticks in a medium bowl and toss them with olive oil. Season generously with the salt and pepper.

- Remove the baking sheets from the oven and coat them with cooking spray. Place the prepared potatoes on the baking sheets in a single layer.

- Return the baking sheets to the oven, and bake until the potatoes are golden on the bottom, about 25 minutes. (If using two baking sheets, be certain to rotate the potatoes halfway through cooking.) Turn the potatoes over, and continue cooking until golden on all sides, another 15 minutes. Taste and adjust for seasoning with salt and pepper. Serve immediately.

BUTTERMILK POTATO—RUTABAGA MASH

Makes 6 servings

Russet potatoes are long and slightly rounded with brown, rough skin and lots of small eyes. They are a low-moisture, high-starch potato. Other potatoes to use in this combination mash are Yukon Gold, new potatoes, and round red or round white potatoes.

Rutabaga is a root vegetable that is not a turnip, but often treated like one. The rutabaga, also sold under the name "Swede" or Swedish turnip, belongs to the cabbage family and has a thin, pale yellow skin and orange-colored flesh. Rutabagas are normally sold with a thin waxy coating to prevent them from sprouting while on the grocer's shelf.

1½	pounds russet potatoes, peeled and cut into 2-inch pieces	¼	cup sour cream
		¼	cup buttermilk
¾	pound rutabagas, peeled and cut into 1-inch pieces		Coarse salt and freshly ground black pepper
¼	cup (4 tablespoons) unsalted butter, room temperature	2	tablespoons snipped fresh chives

- Place the potatoes and rutabagas in a large pot of cold, salted water. Bring to a boil over high heat. Reduce the heat to simmer and cook until tender, about 20 minutes.

- Drain the vegetables and return to the pot. Cook the vegetables in the dry pan, stirring constantly, to remove the excess water, 45 to 60 seconds.

- Add the butter, sour cream, and buttermilk. Using a potato masher, mash until smooth. Season to taste with the salt and pepper. Sprinkle with the chives and serve immediately.

LEEK & FENNEL MASHED POTATOES

Makes 6 servings

Leeks look like large green onions or scallions, but have a more complex onion flavor. They're often cooked as a vegetable side dish or used in soups. Leeks grow in sandy soil and the soil has a tendency to collect between the layers. Wash them several times in a sink full of cold water, letting the dirt sink to the bottom and making sure to lift the leeks out of the water—do not pour the leeks through a colander. If you pour the leeks through a colander, you are simply pouring the dirt on top of the leeks.

The leeks and fennel should be cooked until very tender so they will blend nicely with the potatoes. Try adding a couple of cloves of finely chopped garlic if you want to give the dish a little kick.

1½	pounds Yukon Gold potatoes, peeled and quartered
2	medium leeks
2	tablespoons unsalted butter
1	medium fennel bulb, stalks trimmed, bulb halved and thinly sliced
⅓	cup homemade chicken stock or reduced-fat, low-sodium chicken broth
	Coarse salt and freshly ground black pepper
⅔	cup milk, heated, plus more if necessary

- Place the potatoes in a large pot of cold, salted water. Bring to a boil over high heat. Reduce the heat to simmer and cook until tender, about 20 minutes. Drain the potatoes and return to the pot. Cook the potatoes in the dry pan, stirring constantly, to remove the excess water, 45 to 60 seconds. Set aside and keep warm.

- Meanwhile, remove the dark green portion of the leeks. Cut the remaining leeks in quarters lengthwise and thinly slice. Place the leeks in a large bowl of water and swish to allow the sand to fall to the bottom of the bowl. Lift the leeks into a strainer and drain. Repeat the process to rid leeks of any dirt or sand.

- Heat the butter in a large sauté pan over medium-low heat. Add the leeks and cook, stirring occasionally, until slightly softened, about 5 minutes. Add the fennel and cook, stirring occasionally, until softened, about 5 minutes. Add the stock and season with the salt and pepper to taste. Cover and simmer, until the vegetables are completely tender, about 10 minutes. Add the leek-fennel mixture and milk to the potatoes. Using a potato masher, mash until smooth. Taste and adjust for seasoning with salt and pepper. Serve immediately.

DROPPIN' KNOWLEDGE

When you cut a potato and expose the flesh to air, the potato begins to oxidize and turn brown. To prevent this, simply place the cut potatoes in cold water. The only time this is not a good idea is when you want the starch to remain on the potato so they will stick together, like when making a gratin. In that case, you need to slice the potatoes as you are making the dish.

Looks like things are turned around and producer Virginia Willis is trying to sort things out. Marvin's in a Falcons' jersey and Falcons linebacker Chris Draft has on his BBQ gear.

ROASTED ROOT VEGETABLES WITH BALSAMIC VINAIGRETTE

Makes 6 servings

These roasted root vegetables are scented with the flavors of three fresh herbs. There's nothing like cooking with fresh herbs. We're fortunate in the South because we can grow many herbs almost year-round.

Marjoram has soft, small, oval green leaves. It has a bold scent with hints of mint and pepper. Marjoram is similar to oregano, but slightly milder. Thyme is an herb used often in the kitchen. There are more than one hundred varieties of thyme. Most have clusters of tiny green leaves on a thin, woody stem. Rosemary is a highly aromatic herb and has a flavor that might be described as a cross between lemon and pine. Make sure you use fresh herbs for this recipe for the best results.

3	plus 3 tablespoons extra-virgin olive oil	3/4	pound parsnips, peeled, cut into 3/4-inch pieces
1	tablespoon chopped fresh thyme	3/4	pound rutabagas, peeled, cut into 1/2-inch pieces
1	tablespoon chopped fresh marjoram	1	medium red onion, peeled, root left intact, cut into 1/2-inch-thick wedges
1	tablespoon chopped fresh rosemary		Coarse salt and freshly ground black pepper
1	pound medium sweet potatoes, peeled, cut into 2-inch pieces	6	to 8 cherry tomatoes
		2	tablespoons balsamic vinegar
3/4	pound carrots, peeled, cut into 3/4-inch pieces	2	tablespoons chopped fresh parsley

- Position one rack in the top third and the second rack in the bottom third of the oven and preheat to 425°F. Spray two rimmed baking sheets with nonstick spray.

- Whisk 3 tablespoons oil, thyme, marjoram, and rosemary in a large bowl. Add the sweet potatoes, carrots, parsnips, rutabagas, and onion and toss to coat. Season generously with the salt and pepper and divide between the prepared baking sheets. Roast the vegetables until tender, turning occasionally, about 50 minutes. Add the cherry tomatoes and cook until heated through, about 10 minutes.

- Whisk the balsamic vinegar and remaining 3 tablespoons oil in a small bowl. Drizzle over the roasted vegetables. Taste, adjust for seasoning with the salt and pepper, and toss. Sprinkle with the parsley. Serve hot or at room temperature.

PORK

Outside of the South pork is completely misunderstood. The reputation of pork was so poor that the pork counsel had to come up with that funny little slogan about pork being the other white meat to boost sales and make folks aware of how tasty and often overlooked it is.

In the South, however, if pork were a person it could run for mayor and win by a landslide! Once, when I visited my Aunt Tiny in North Carolina, she fixed a breakfast for me (let me remind you I grew up in the North) of eggs, grits, pork chops, and gravy. Yes, pork chops for breakfast. Can I just say, **Oh my gosh!** I thought I had died and gone to heaven. That meal made such an impact on me that it began my never-ending love for pork.

Since there is a myth out there that pork must be cooked until it resembles a boot, and that it can't be served pink. There is nothing further from the truth. You don't have to take my word for it. Do some research; you'll find that pork can be eaten and enjoyed at medium temperature now. You will also find out that there hasn't been a case of trichinoses in over fifty years. Pork is raised and bred using techniques completely different from the days of our grandparents. I encourage you to cook a piece around the medium stage and see what you think.

MUSTARD & HERB-CRUSTED ROAST PORK

Makes 6 to 8 servings

The herb-mustard crust on the pork seals in the juices and guarantees a juicy roast. That is if you don't overcook it. Pale pink is fine in pork. Today's farming methods have virtually eradicated the threat of trichinosis.

Mustard packs a whole lot of flavor without a lot of fat. Dijon mustard is made from the husked, black seeds blended with wine, salt, and spices. It is pale yellow and varies from mild to very hot. Coarse-grain mustard is also known as whole-grain or country-style. In a country known for great food and wine, the Burgundy region of France has a great culinary history. Dijon, France, was home to the powerful dukes of Burgundy. The dukes were as rich and powerful as the French kings and demanded the very best food for their guests and the very best wine to complement it. Lots of money, lots of wine . . . and lots of mustard.

6	tablespoons whole-grain Dijon mustard
6	garlic cloves, finely chopped
4	bay leaves, finely crushed
3	tablespoons olive oil
3	tablespoons balsamic vinegar
1	tablespoon chopped fresh rosemary
1	tablespoon chopped fresh sage
1	(2½-pound) boneless pork rib roast
	Coarse salt and freshly ground black pepper

- Preheat the oven to 375°F. In a small bowl combine the mustard, garlic, bay leaves, olive oil, vinegar, rosemary, and sage.

- Pat the pork dry with paper towels. Season liberally with the salt and pepper. Spread the mustard mixture all over pork. (You can marinate the pork in a sealable plastic container in the refrigerator overnight for even greater mustard flavor.)

- Place the pork on a rack set in a roasting pan. Transfer to the oven and roast the pork until a thermometer inserted into center registers 150°F, about 1 hour. Remove from the oven and let stand 10 minutes before slicing. As it rests, the juices will redistribute and the temperature will continue to rise, about 5 degrees. Serve immediately.

DROPPIN' KNOWLEDGE

It is not recommended to thaw foods at room temperature. This causes bacteria to multiply more rapidly. The best method of thawing is in the refrigerator for 24 to 48 hours or to completely submerge the food in 70°F water.

ROAST PORK
WITH CABBAGE & CARAWAY

Makes 6 servings

Southern Sundays call out for a family meal with everyone around the table. And southerners love pork. This Roast Pork with Cabbage and Caraway is a great Sunday dinner recipe, good all year, but especially delicious in the fall and winter months. Serve alone with warm biscuits to sop up the sauce or sauté sliced apples as a garnish.

Caraway seeds are small, tannish brown seeds that have a flavor similar to a blend of dill and fennel—sweet, but faintly sharp. Caraway seed is known for its flavor in rye bread, and it is used to flavor cakes, biscuits, cheese, sauerkraut, and potato dishes. Caraway marries very nicely with pork and cabbage.

2	plus 1 plus 1 teaspoons caraway seeds, crushed
2	large garlic cloves, finely chopped
	Coarse salt and freshly ground black pepper
1	(3-pound) boneless, center-cut loin pork roast
1	plus 1 plus 1 tablespoon olive oil
1	large onion, sliced
4	carrots, peeled and sliced on the diagonal
2	bay leaves
1	(2½-pound) head green cabbage, quartered, cored and sliced
1½	cups apple juice
2	tablespoons unsulphured molasses
½	cup homemade chicken stock or reduced-fat, low-sodium chicken broth

ROAST PORK
WITH CABBAGE & CARAWAY

(continued)

- Combine 2 teaspoons caraway seeds, garlic, and salt and pepper to taste in a small bowl. Place the pork in a glass baking dish. Rub the pork with the spice mixture. Cover and chill in the refrigerator up to 24 hours.

- Preheat the oven to 350°F. Heat 1 tablespoon olive oil in a large Dutch oven over medium-high heat. Add the onion, carrots, bay leaves, and 1 teaspoon caraway seeds. Sauté until softened, about 8 minutes. Transfer to a large bowl and set aside.

- Heat 1 tablespoon oil in the same pan over high heat. Add the cabbage and the remaining 1 teaspoon caraway seeds. Sauté until the cabbage begins to wilt, about 5 minutes. Add the cabbage to the onion mixture. Stir to combine. Season with the salt and pepper.

- Remove the pork from the refrigerator. Heat the remaining 1 tablespoon oil in the same pan over high heat. Add the pork and sear to brown on all sides, about 10 minutes.

- Remove the pork to a plate. Add the apple juice, molasses, and chicken stock to the pan. Bring to a boil, scraping up any browned bits. Return the vegetables and the pork to the pan. Season with more salt and pepper.

- Cover with a tight-fitting lid and transfer to the oven. Roast the pork and vegetables until an instant-read thermometer reads 150°F, 45 minutes to 1 hour. Remove the pork and set aside to rest for 10 minutes before slicing.

- Remove and discard the bay leaves. Taste and adjust for seasoning with the salt and pepper. Using a slotted spoon, place the vegetables on the platter. Bring the remaining juices to a boil and reduce slightly, about 5 minutes. Slice the pork and place atop the vegetables. Spoon the pan sauce over the pork and serve immediately.

PORK CHOPS
WITH CILANTRO & CUMIN

Makes 4 servings

The spice coriander is a tannish brown seed and has a sweet, aromatic, slightly lemony flavor. Coriander is actually thought to increase the appetite. It is often used in Mediterranean, North African, Mexican, Indian, and Southeast Asian cuisines, as well as spice blends, including curry powders, chili powders, and garam masala. Cilantro is the usual name for the leaf of the plant from which coriander seed is obtained. Cilantro, also known as fresh coriander or Chinese parsley, has a distinctive green, waxy flavor.

Spices such as coriander and cumin seed should be toasted to intensify their flavors. Simply add the spice to a dry, nonstick, heated skillet and heat until aromatic, just a couple of minutes then grind in a small electric coffee grinder (designated for spices) or use a mortar and pestle. Ground spices release their flavor more quickly than whole spices.

2	tablespoons cumin seed, toasted and coarsely ground
2	tablespoons coriander, toasted and coarsely ground
4	garlic cloves, finely chopped
2	plus 2 tablespoons olive oil
4	pork chops, cut ¾ inch thick
	Coarse salt and freshly ground black pepper
3	tablespoons chopped fresh cilantro
1	lime, quartered for garnish

- Using a small bowl, combine the cumin, coriander, garlic, and 2 tablespoons olive oil. Pat the pork chops dry and season with the salt and pepper to taste. Rub the spice mixture on both sides of chops.

- Using a large, heavy-bottom sauté pan over medium heat, heat the remaining 2 tablespoons olive oil until hot but not smoking. Cook the chops until browned and cooked through, about 6 minutes on each side. Sprinkle with the cilantro and serve with the lime wedges.

BOURBON-BAKED HAM

Makes 10 servings

Ham comes from the hind leg of the hog. Ham can be fresh, cured, or cured and smoked. Fresh ham is pale pink and beige in color after cooking. Cured ham is usually deep pink in color as a result of the curing process. Dry-cured ham like country ham and prosciutto is deep pink to mahogany red in color.

Hams are available bone-in or boneless. Bone-in hams are more flavorful than boneless hams. Bone-in hams will have part of the leg bone or hipbone intact, plus some smaller bones depending on the cut. You can purchase a whole ham (pretty much the entire leg of the hog) that will feed an army, or you can buy a half ham. Half hams come in two varieties: the butt end and the shank end. The butt end comes from the upper thigh and has a rounded end, whereas the shank end comes from the lower portion of the leg and has a pointed or tapered end.

1	cup honey
½	cup molasses
½	cup bourbon
¼	cup freshly squeezed orange juice
2	tablespoons Dijon mustard
1	(6 to 8-pound) cured ham half

- Preheat the oven to 350°F. Lightly grease a medium roasting pan with nonstick spray.

- Heat the honey, molasses, bourbon, orange juice, and mustard in a medium pot over medium heat until melted and combined.

- Remove the skin and fat from ham. Using a sharp knife make ¼-inch-deep cuts in the ham in a diamond pattern.

- Place the ham in the prepared roasting pan. Pour the honey glaze over the ham. Transfer to the oven and bake for 2 to 2½ hours or until a meat thermometer inserted into the thickest portion registers 140°F, basting every 30 minutes or so with the glaze on the bottom of the pan. When done, remove the ham to a rack and transfer it to a cutting board. Cover the ham loosely with aluminum foil to keep warm.

- Remove and discard the excess fat from the collected drippings in the bottom of the roasting pan. Transfer the drippings to a small saucepan. Bring the drippings to a boil. Slice the ham and serve with the warm drippings.

DROPPIN' KNOWLEDGE

When measuring out sticky ingredients such as honey, spray a little nonstick spray into the measuring utensil and it will help the sticky ingredient to slide right out.

SLOW COOKER PORK CHOPS WITH DRIED APPLES

Makes 6 servings

Apples go with pork chops like bread goes with butter, salt with pepper, and milk with cookies. The sweet taste of the apple juice combined with brown sugar and dried apples is perfect with these tender slow-cooked chops. You'll really appreciate this meal after a long day at work.

Cooking juices won't naturally thicken in a slow cooker, so you have to use a thickening agent such as cornstarch. Cornstarch will form lumps if added directly to a hot liquid. So, combine it with a small amount of cold water before stirring it into the hot mixture. This is called a slurry. Sauces thickened with cornstarch will be clear and glossy.

¾	cup apple juice	½	cup fresh or dried cranberries
½	cup firmly packed dark brown sugar	1	large onion, chopped
	Coarse salt and freshly ground black pepper	2	celery stalks, sliced into ½-inch pieces
2	pounds pork chops	1½	tablespoons cornstarch
1	cup chopped dried apple	2	tablespoons cold water

- Combine the apple juice and brown sugar in a medium bowl. Season with the salt and pepper to taste.

- Place the pork, dried apple, cranberries, onion, and celery in the insert of the slow cooker. Season with more salt and pepper. Add the apple juice mixture and stir to combine.

- To complete in a slow cooker, cover and cook on low for 7 to 9 hours or on high 3 to 4 hours.

- Thirty minutes before serving, remove the solids to a large shallow bowl. Tent the bowl loosely with foil to keep warm. Transfer the liquid to a separate container and skim off the excess fat.

- Combine the cornstarch and water. Stir in the cornstarch mixture and return the cooking liquid to the slow cooker. Continue cooking on low for another 20 to 30 minutes until slightly thickened. Taste and adjust for seasoning with salt and pepper. Pour over the stewed pork and apples and serve immediately.

FETTUCCINI WITH COUNTRY HAM & SUN-DRIED TOMATOES

Makes 4 to 6 servings

Virginia was an early hub for ham production, particularly in the town of Smithfield. The other main country-ham-producing states are Tennessee, Kentucky, and North Carolina. The major difference between one country ham and another is less due to geography and more a result of the style of the individual producer.

The basic method for making all country hams is the same. The hind leg of the pig is generously rubbed with salt, which cures the meat. Many country ham producers also use sugar, which not only sweetens the meat but also helps to tenderize it. Most also use saltpeter (potassium nitrate) which acts as a preservative and gives the ham a rich color. Once the ham is cured, it is aged in an 80°F, 60 percent humidity room for a minimum of 25 days and up to 120 to 150 days.

1	pound fettuccini	2	cups heavy cream
2	tablespoons unsalted butter	4	ounces country ham, cut into strips
1	onion, chopped	2½	cups peas, not thawed if frozen
1	garlic clove, very finely chopped		Freshly ground black pepper
4	ounces sun-dried tomatoes, diced	2	tablespoons chopped fresh parsley

- Cook the pasta in a large pot of rapidly boiling, salted water until al dente, 8 to 10 minutes or according to package instructions.

- Meanwhile, melt the butter in a large skillet over medium-low heat. Add the onion and cook until translucent, about 5 minutes. Add the garlic and cook until fragrant, 45 to 60 seconds. Add the diced tomatoes and cream. Simmer, stirring frequently, until reduced, about 5 minutes. Just before the pasta finishes cooking, add the ham strips and peas to the cream sauce to warm through. Season to taste with pepper and keep warm. (The sauce will not need salt since the ham is already quite salty.)

- Drain the pasta. Add to the cream-ham mixture and toss to coat. Taste and adjust for seasoning with salt and pepper. Transfer to a warm platter and sprinkle with the chopped parsley. Serve immediately.

ROAST PORK WITH DRIED PEACHES & PLUMS

Makes 6 to 8 servings

Today's hogs are raised leaner, meeting the demand for quality pork with less fat. The loin is where we get the leanest and most tender pork cuts. Since they're lean, these cuts tend to dry out if overcooked. On average, cook pork loin about 20 minutes per pound for meat that is not overcooked and dry.

Pork is safe to eat if it's cooked to an interior temperature of 150°F—the meat will continue to cook and the temperature will rise to 160°F as it rests out of the oven. There are three main parts of the loin: the blade end, which is closest to the shoulder and tends to be fatty; the sirloin end, which is closest to the rump and tends to be bony; and the center portion in the middle, which is lean, tender, and a little more expensive.

1	(4-pound) boneless, center-cut pork loin roast	3/4	plus 1/4 cup freshly squeezed orange juice
	Coarse salt and freshly ground black pepper	1	cup dried peaches
1/4	cup Dijon mustard	1	cup dried plums
2	plus 2 tablespoons firmly packed brown sugar	3/4	cup port wine
		1/8	teaspoon allspice
		2	teaspoons cornstarch

- Preheat the oven to 350°F. Season the pork liberally with salt and pepper. Combine the mustard and 2 tablespoons brown sugar in a small bowl. Spread the mixture over the pork loin. Place the pork in shallow roasting pan. Transfer to the oven and roast the pork until an instant-read thermometer reads 150°F, 1 to 1½ hours.

- Meanwhile combine the remaining 2 tablespoons brown sugar, 3/4 cup orange juice, dried peaches, dried plums, port, and allspice in a saucepan. Bring to a boil over high heat. Cover and reduce the heat to low. Simmer until the fruit is plump, about 15 minutes.

- Spoon the fruit mixture around the pork roast during the last 30 minutes of the roasting time.

- Remove from the oven and transfer the roast and fruits to a serving platter. The pan juices will remain. Tent the pork with foil to keep warm. Set aside to rest for 10 minutes before slicing.

- Combine the remaining 1/4 cup orange juice and cornstarch. Gradually whisk the orange juice mixture into the pan juices, stirring until slightly thickened. Taste and adjust for seasoning with salt and pepper. Serve the sauce over the sliced roast and serve immediately.

[SEE PHOTO ON PAGE 136]

QUICK & EASY PULLED-PORK SANDWICHES

Makes 4 to 6 servings

Barbecue is veritably a religion in the South. There is very little in the realm of southern food that stirs deeper emotions. The sight of a perfectly smoked, sauced, and seasoned slab of ribs or a mound of steaming hot pulled pork is practically grail-like.

This recipe is not traditional, but unless you have time to dig a pit, it's the one for barbecue at home. The shortcut is using pork tenderloin. Pork tenderloin is lean, tender, boneless, and cooks quickly. It is located on either side of the backbone adjacent to the short ribs just below the loin. If there's a silver membrane on the tenderloin, remove it before cooking. For this recipe to work best, it is important to get a good sear on the tenderloin before coating it with sauce and putting it in the oven.

1	plus 1 tablespoons olive oil
1	small onion, finely chopped
1	small red bell pepper, seeded and finely chopped
1	celery stalk, very finely chopped
1½	cups ketchup
¾	cup firmly packed dark brown sugar
2	tablespoons yellow mustard
2	tablespoons Dijon mustard
	Juice of 1 lemon
2	tablespoons Worcestershire sauce
1	tablespoon garlic powder
¼	teaspoon chili powder
¼	teaspoon cayenne (or to taste)
	Coarse salt and freshly ground black pepper
1	(16-ounce) pork tenderloin, trimmed of excess fat and silver skin
4	to 6 hamburger buns

- Heat 1 tablespoon olive oil in a medium saucepan over medium heat. Add the onion, bell pepper, and celery. Cook until tender, stirring occasionally, about 5 minutes. Add the ketchup and brown sugar and stir to combine. Reduce the heat to low. Simmer, stirring occasionally, until the sugar is completely dissolved. Add the yellow and Dijon mustards, lemon juice, Worcestershire sauce, garlic powder, chili powder, and cayenne. Cover and continue to cook, stirring occasionally, until thickened, about 30 minutes. Season with the salt and pepper to taste. (Add water as needed for a sauce-like consistency.)

- Preheat the oven to 350°F. Line a baking sheet with aluminum foil. Set aside.

- Heat the remaining 1 tablespoon olive oil in a medium skillet over medium-high heat. Season the pork with salt and pepper. Sear the tenderloin on all sides, 5 to 7 minutes.

- Remove from the heat and transfer to the prepared sheet pan. Top the pork tenderloin with one-third of the sauce, rolling to coat. Fold the top and ends of foil to form a tight seal.

- Bake the pork in the oven until tender, about 30 minutes. Transfer the pork to a large bowl. Discard any remaining cooking juices. Using two forks shred the pork tenderloin into fine strips. Add the sauce to coat, about 1 cup. Taste and adjust for seasoning with salt and pepper. Serve on the split buns with remaining sauce on the side.

CHICKEN
& POULTRY

The South is no longer just about fried chicken and cornbread. Modern southern food is influenced by a wide variety of flavors and cuisines.

One thing that I really enjoy doing is turning people on to something new. These next few pages will hopefully do just that, with recipes from turkey, to quail, to of course, chicken. How about Roasted Orange-Herb Cornish Game Hens or Oven-Fried Pecan-Crusted Chicken Breasts? Step out with Crispy Duck Breasts with Port-Cherry Reduction!

Read on and understand that these recipes are not run-of-the-mill and might require a sense of adventure.

RED WINE CHICKEN WITH MUSHROOMS

Makes 4 to 6 servings

Slow cookers properly used are a great way to reap the benefits of long, slow cooking. The direct heat combined with bacteria-killing steam created inside the tightly covered container help keep foods safe. When buying a slow cooker, you'll find that there are a lot of options available to you. Look for one that has a removable liner. This feature is nice for both cleaning purposes and transporting food. This slow cooker recipe is a fresh twist on chicken stew using skinless, boneless chicken thighs.

To thicken the cooking juices, this recipe uses quick-cooking tapioca. Tapioca is a starch obtained from the cassava or yucca plant. Most often we see it in pellets in desserts like tapioca pudding, but it is also available in flakes, pellets, and flour. Tapioca is available in most supermarkets and grocery stores.

3	pounds skinless, boneless chicken thighs
	Coarse salt and freshly ground black pepper
12	ounces white button mushrooms, sliced
1	large onion, chopped
3	garlic cloves, finely chopped
3/4	cup homemade chicken stock or reduced-fat, low-sodium chicken broth
1	(6-ounce) can tomato paste
1/4	cup dry red wine
2	tablespoons quick-cooking tapioca
2	teaspoons sugar
2	tablespoons chopped fresh basil
	Cooked egg noodles for serving
	Freshly grated Parmigiano-Reggiano cheese for serving

- Season the thighs with the salt and pepper. Place the mushrooms, onion, and garlic in the insert of the slow cooker. Place the seasoned chicken pieces on top of the vegetables.

- Combine the stock, tomato paste, wine, tapioca, and sugar in a medium bowl. Season with salt and pepper. Pour the stock mixture over the chicken and vegetables.

- Cover and cook on low for 7 to 8 hours or high for 3½ to 4 hours until the chicken is cooked and tender.

- Just before serving, add the basil and stir to combine. Taste and adjust for seasoning with salt and pepper. Serve the chicken on a bed of cooked egg noodles and top with Parmigiano-Reggiano cheese.

DROPPIN' KNOWLEDGE

Bacteria grow in temperatures between 41°F and 140°F. This range is known as the "danger zone". If certain foods are left out for too long in the danger zone, they can be potentially dangerous including the obvious such as poultry, fish, shellfish, beef, pork, soy-protein products, and lamb. Even some cooked products can be dangerous including cooked rice, baked, and boiled potatoes, sliced melons, garlic and oil mixtures, cooked beans, and pasta.

ROASTED ORANGE-HERB CORNISH GAME HENS

Makes 4 servings

Those little birds that aren't quite a chicken but larger than quail are called Cornish game hens or Rock Cornish hens. They are best broiled or roasted. This recipe benefits from citrus herb butter and a pan sauce made with sherry. The sauce is finished on the stovetop, so make sure to use a roasting pan that can go directly on the heat. Otherwise, use a large, ovenproof skillet.

Sherry is a Spanish-style fortified wine from the *Jerez de la Frontera* region. Sherries can range from sweet to dry, and are served either at room temperature or chilled. Sherries range in color, flavor, and sweetness. They are most often consumed as an aperitif. In cooking, sherry adds a lively sweet flavor. First and foremost when cooking with wine, never use a wine labeled "cooking wine." Don't cook with anything you would not drink. Cooking wines are full of sodium and don't taste anything like the real thing.

5	tablespoons chopped fresh mixed herbs such as thyme, rosemary, and parsley		Coarse salt and freshly ground black pepper
3	shallots, chopped	1	cup homemade chicken stock or reduced-fat, low-sodium chicken broth
1	tablespoon grated orange zest		
2	Cornish game hens, halved lengthwise (about 1½ pounds each)	½	cup freshly squeezed orange juice
¼	cup (½ stick) unsalted butter, room temperature	¼	cup dry sherry
		4	thin orange slices for garnish

- Preheat the oven to 450°F. Combine half the herbs, the shallots, and orange zest in a small bowl. Gently loosen the skin of the hen halves by sliding fingers between the skin and meat.

- Spread 2 teaspoons of the herb mixture under the skin of each hen half. Rub each skin with 1 tablespoon butter. Season with the salt and pepper to taste. Place the hens in a shallow, heatproof roasting pan.

- Transfer the pan to the oven and roast the hens 10 minutes. Add the stock to the pan and baste the hens. Continue roasting until golden brown and cooked through, an additional 20 minutes, basting halfway through.

- Transfer the hen halves to a platter. Place the roasting pan over medium heat. Add the orange juice, sherry, and the remaining herb mixture. Bring to a boil, scraping up the browned bits. Reduce until thickened, about 2 minutes. Taste and adjust for seasoning with salt and pepper. Spoon the sauce over the hens. Garnish with orange slices and serve immediately.

GLORIFIED TURKEY BURGERS

Makes 4 servings

At The Varsity drive-in in Atlanta, Georgia, the staff has a language all their own. They bellow, "What'llyahave? What'llyahave?" as you get to the head of the line. Founded in 1928, The Varsity is the world's largest drive-in restaurant, selling more Coca-Cola than any other single outlet in the world. The menu includes hot dogs, chili dogs, hamburgers, chiliburgers, onion rings, and French fries.

If you say, "French fries," the counterman calls out, "Strings!" to those who assemble the orders. A hamburger with mustard is a "Yankee steak," referring to its yellow streak, and onions on the side make it "sideways." A "glorified steak" is a hamburger with mayonnaise, lettuce, and tomato. In the healthy Home Plate way, here's a recipe for turkey burgers. You won't miss the fat, just maybe the "What'llyahave?"

1½	cups fresh white breadcrumbs
½	Vidalia onion, very finely chopped
1	tablespoon canola oil
½	teaspoon salt
¼	teaspoon freshly ground black pepper
1½	pounds ground turkey meat
4	slices Cheddar cheese (optional)
4	buns, warmed
	Lettuce, sliced tomato, sliced red onion, pickle for serving
	Ketchup, mustard, mayonnaise for serving

- Combine the breadcrumbs, onion, canola oil, salt, pepper, and ground turkey in a medium bowl. Mix with your hands until well blended. Form the mixture into four patties.

- Heat a grill pan or griddle over medium-high heat. Place the patties on the grill pan. Cook 3 to 5 minutes per side until the juices run clear when poked with a knife. Once patties are flipped, top each with a slice of the cheese. Transfer the burgers to the warmed buns. Serve immediately with a choice of toppings.

OVEN-FRIED PECAN-CRUSTED CHICKEN STRIPS

Makes 4 servings

In this recipe the most important ingredient is the buttermilk. The acid content of the buttermilk lends a tenderizing effect when marinating poultry, meat, or fish. Once upon a time, buttermilk was nothing more than the tart liquid left after butter was churned. Now it is made by adding special bacteria to nonfat or low-fat milk.

One problem with buttermilk is it seems to always come in quart containers—when you need only a couple of cups. To substitute use one tablespoon freshly squeezed lemon juice or cider vinegar to one cup milk and let stand five minutes at room temperature.

1	tablespoon canola oil
4	skinless, boneless chicken breasts (about $1\frac{1}{2}$ pounds)
$\frac{1}{2}$	cup buttermilk
$\frac{1}{4}$	cup Dijon mustard
	Coarse salt and freshly ground black pepper
$1\frac{1}{2}$	cups finely chopped pecans

- Preheat the oven to 375°F. Oil a baking sheet. Rinse the chicken breasts and pat them dry. Using a sharp knife, cut the breasts into $\frac{1}{2}$-inch strips.

- In a medium bowl combine the buttermilk, mustard, and salt and pepper to taste. Add the chicken strips and turn to coat well. Refrigerate and marinate for 15 minutes, stirring occasionally.

- Place the pecans on a plate. Season the pecans with salt and pepper. Remove the chicken strips from the buttermilk, shaking off the excess. Roll the strips in the seasoned pecans and place them on the prepared baking sheet. Bake in the oven until browned and the juices run clear when pierced with a knife, 20 to 25 minutes. Serve immediately.

DROPPIN' KNOWLEDGE

All nuts, including pecans, will go rancid if not stored in the proper environment. To keep nuts fresh, store them in the refrigerator or freezer. Pecans can be frozen and refrozen in an airtight container for up to two years without loss of flavor or texture. Buy enough for the year in the fall when they are in season and put them in the freezer. You'll be glad you did!

PAN-FRIED CHICKEN BREASTS WITH OREGANO BUTTER

Makes 4 servings

This recipe uses an herb butter to flavor and moisten the chicken breasts. We start with unsalted butter and add herbs, spices, and salt. It may seem confusing to add salt to recipes that call for unsalted butter, but this way you are able to control the amount of salt in the dish. It is much better to add the seasoning with your own hand than to rely on an outside source, since different brands vary in salt content.

Also, butter is regulated and graded by the amount of butterfat it contains. The higher the butterfat, the higher the grade it is awarded. Salted butter is often made from a lower-grade butter. In fact, salt has been used for centuries to conceal off flavors. Unsalted butter, also known as sweet butter, is best for all recipes—savory and sweet.

2	garlic cloves, finely chopped		Coarse salt and freshly ground black pepper
5	tablespoons unsalted butter, room temperature	1	cup all-purpose flour
1	tablespoon chopped fresh oregano	4	chicken breast halves, skin on, bone in (about 2 pounds)
½	teaspoon red pepper flakes	2	tablespoons olive oil

- Combine the garlic, butter, oregano, and red pepper flakes in a small bowl. Season with the salt and pepper to taste. Place the flour in a shallow plate and season with salt and pepper.

- Rinse the chicken breasts and pat them dry. Using a sharp knife, cut a 2-inch-long pocket horizontally in each chicken breast half. Fill each pocket with about 2 teaspoons of the oregano butter. (Do not let the measuring spoon touch the raw chicken so as to contaminate the oregano butter since you will serve the remaining butter on the side at the end of cooking.) Season the chicken with salt and pepper. Lightly coat it in the seasoned flour, shaking to remove the excess.

- Heat the oil in a large skillet over medium-high heat until hot but not smoking. Add the chicken, skin side down, and cook until well browned, about 8 minutes. Turn the chicken over, reduce the heat to medium, cover the skillet, and cook until the juices run clear when pierced with a knife, about 10 minutes.

- Serve immediately with the remaining oregano butter on the side.

ROSEMARY ROAST TURKEY

Makes 12 servings

Simple roast turkey is a holiday tradition. But don't get caught in a pinch the day of the big feast with a frozen bird. If you buy a frozen turkey, refrigerator thawing is recommended. (Thawing the turkey at room temperature is not recommended since it could promote bacterial growth and lead to food-borne illness.) To thaw a whole turkey in the refrigerator, place the turkey in its unopened wrapper, breast side up, on a tray. For every four pounds of turkey, allow at least one day of thawing.

If you are short on time, submerge the turkey in cold water. Place the turkey in its unopened wrapper, breast down, and cover completely with cold water. Change the water every thirty minutes to keep the surface of the turkey cold. The thawing time in cold water is about thirty minutes per pound for a whole turkey.

DROPPIN' KNOWLEDGE

Cross contamination is the transfer of microorganisms from one place, or food, to another, and it can make you sick. It occurs by improper handling of foods like fresh produce, raw meat, poultry, and seafood. The best prevention of cross contamination is to keep these foods separated. Always use a clean cutting board for fresh produce and a separate clean cutting board for raw meat, poultry, and seafood.

FOR THE TURKEY:

1 (12 to 14-pound) turkey
6 large fresh bay leaves
1 bunch fresh rosemary sprigs
1 apple, quartered
1 celery stalk, halved
1 onion, halved
½ cup unsalted butter, melted, more for the pan
Coarse salt and freshly ground black pepper

FOR THE GRAVY:

2 tablespoons unsalted butter
2 tablespoons all-purpose flour
4 cups turkey drippings, fat removed, and homemade chicken stock or reduced-fat, low-sodium chicken broth
Coarse salt and freshly ground black pepper

(continued)

- Preheat the oven to 325°F. Lightly grease a broiler or roasting pan with melted butter. Remove the neck and giblets from the turkey. Rinse the turkey in cold water and drain. Pat dry and place the turkey with the wing tips tucked under the bird in the prepared pan.

- Without detaching the skin, carefully loosen the skin from the turkey breast. Slip several bay leaves and rosemary sprigs underneath the skin. In the body cavity of the turkey place the apple quarters, celery, onion, and the remaining bay leaves and rosemary sprigs.

- Brush the bird with the remaining melted butter and lightly cover with heavy-duty aluminum foil. Transfer to the oven and bake, basting frequently during cooking with drippings from pan, until an instant-read thermometer registers 180°F when inserted into the meaty part of the thigh, 3 to 4 hours. Cook the turkey uncovered during the last hour of cooking. (The juices should be clear, not reddish pink, when the thigh muscle is pierced with a knife.)

- Begin checking for doneness after 3 hours. Once finished, remove the turkey from the pan and let stand for 15 minutes, reserving the pan drippings for the gravy.

- For the gravy, in a large saucepan over medium heat melt the butter until foaming. Add the flour and cook, stirring constantly, about 3 minutes. Whisk in the reserved turkey drippings plus enough stock to make 4 cups. Increase the heat to high and bring to a boil. Reduce the heat to simmer and cook until the gravy is thick enough to coat the back of a wooden spoon, about 15 minutes. Taste and adjust the seasoning with salt and pepper. Serve the sliced turkey with the gravy on the side.

TURKEY MEATLOAF

Makes 6 servings

Balance, variety, and moderation are the keys to a healthful diet. You don't have to sacrifice good taste for good health. Modifying recipes by substituting low-fat foods for higher-fat ones is the best way to skim the fat. Here we turn traditional meatloaf into a more healthful entrée by switching from ground beef to ground turkey.

Adding mushrooms to the mix adds flavor and texture without adding fat. Cremini mushrooms are simply baby portobello mushrooms. They are dark brown and slightly firmer and more full-flavored than white button mushrooms. Look for mushrooms with no bruises, closed gills, and a rounded cap that ranges from one-half to two inches in diameter. If you cannot find cremini, plain white button mushrooms may be substituted.

2	tablespoons olive oil, plus more for pan	2	teaspoons Worcestershire sauce
1	large onion, finely chopped	½	cup chopped fresh parsley
1	medium carrot, finely diced	¼	cup ketchup
12	ounces cremini mushrooms, finely diced	1	cup fresh white breadcrumbs
	Coarse salt and freshly ground black pepper	⅓	cup milk
		2	large eggs, lightly beaten
2	garlic cloves, finely chopped	1¼	pounds ground turkey meat (mix of dark and light)

- Preheat the oven to 400°F. Oil a 13 x 9 x 2-inch loaf pan.

- Heat the oil in a large sauté pan over medium heat. Add the onion and cook, stirring, just until softened, about 2 minutes. Add the carrot and cook, stirring, until softened, about 3 minutes. Add the mushrooms, season with salt and pepper to taste, and cook, stirring occasionally, until the liquid mushrooms give off is evaporated, 10 to 12 minutes. Add the garlic and cook until fragrant, 45 to 60 seconds. Remove from the heat and add Worcestershire sauce, parsley, and ketchup. Transfer the vegetables to a large bowl to cool.

- In a small bowl combine the breadcrumbs and milk, and let stand 5 minutes. Add the eggs and stir to combine. Add the breadcrumb mixture to the cooled vegetables. Add the turkey, season with salt and pepper, and mix well with your hands. Mixture will be very moist.

- Form into a 9 x 5-inch oval loaf and place in the prepared pan. Transfer to the oven, and bake until an instant-read thermometer inserted into the center registers 170°F, about 50 minutes. Remove to a rack to cool and tent loosely with foil. Let the meatloaf stand 5 minutes before serving.

PARMESAN CHICKEN BREASTS

Makes 4 servings

In a rush? Need to get dinner on the table in a hurry? This simple recipe is great for you. Skinless, boneless chicken breasts are a great time-saver, but all too often they are dry and tough. These chicken breasts are coated with a tangy breading with Dijon mustard and Parmesan that locks in the flavor.

Like all fresh meats, chicken is perishable and should be handled with care. Refrigerate raw chicken promptly. Never leave it on the countertop at room temperature or in a hot car while you are shopping.

¼	cup Dijon mustard
2	teaspoons red wine vinegar
	Coarse salt and freshly ground black pepper
4	whole, skinless, boneless chicken breasts (about 1½ pounds)
1½	English muffins
¾	cup freshly grated Parmigiano-Reggiano cheese
2	tablespoons unsalted butter, melted

- Preheat the oven to 450°F. Line a baking sheet with parchment paper.

- In a large bowl whisk together the mustard and vinegar. Season with the salt and pepper to taste. Add the chicken breasts and toss to coat.

- Using a food processor fitted with a blade attachment, pulse the English muffins until finely ground. Add the cheese, butter, and salt and pepper to taste and pulse until combined. Transfer the breading to a shallow dish.

- Remove the chicken from the marinade, and dredge in the seasoned crumbs, coating completely and pressing crumbs to adhere. Transfer the breasts to the prepared baking sheet. Transfer to the oven and bake until golden brown and the juices run clear when pierced with a knife, 20 to 25 minutes. Check after 15 minutes. If the chicken is getting too brown, reduce the heat to 400°F, and add 5 minutes to the total cooking time. Serve immediately.

[SEE PHOTO ON PAGE 150]

CHICKEN BREASTS WITH HERB PAN SAUCE

Makes 4 servings

Cooking bone-in, skin-on chicken breasts can be a problem. They are difficult to cook through on the stovetop, and it's tricky to get crisp skin with moist meat in the oven. Pan-roasting is a restaurant technique in which food is browned in a skillet on the stovetop and then finished in a hot oven. In this recipe the skillet is then deglazed with stock and vermouth to make a quick pan sauce.

Although used perhaps more often in martinis, dry vermouth is also used in cooking. All vermouths, both white and red, are made from white wine that is flavored with aromatic herbal extracts and spices and fortified with spirits. Dry vermouth is white, contains less sugar than red vermouth, and can be served as an aperitif. White vermouth is most often used for cooking and can be substituted for dry white wine.

4	bone-in, skin-on chicken breasts (about 2 pounds)	¾	cup homemade chicken stock or reduced-fat, low-sodium chicken broth
	Coarse salt and freshly ground black pepper	2	to 3 sprigs chopped fresh herbs, such as thyme, sage, or parsley
2	tablespoons canola or vegetable oil		
1	large shallot, finely chopped	2	tablespoons unsalted butter, cut into pieces
½	cup dry vermouth		

- Adjust the oven rack to lowest position and preheat to 450°F.

- Season the chicken with the salt and pepper to taste. In a large, heavy-bottom ovenproof skillet over medium-high heat, heat the oil until it begins to smoke. Add the chicken skin side down and cook until deep golden, about 5 minutes. Turn and brown until golden on the other side, about 3 minutes. Return the chicken to skin side down and transfer to the oven.

- Roast until the juices run clear when the chicken is pierced with a knife, about 15 minutes. Transfer the chicken to a platter, and let rest while making the sauce.

- Remove all but a couple of tablespoons of the fat from the skillet and place over medium heat. Add the shallot and sauté, stirring frequently, until softened, about 2 minutes. Add the vermouth, chicken stock, and herbs. Increase the heat to high, scraping the skillet with a wooden spoon to loosen the browned bits.

- Cook until the sauce is slightly thickened, about 5 minutes. Pour any accumulated chicken juices into the skillet and reduce the heat to medium. Remove from the heat and whisk in the butter one piece at a time. Taste and adjust for seasoning with salt and pepper. Spoon the sauce over the chicken breasts and serve immediately.

OVEN-FRIED CHICKEN LEGS

Makes 4 servings

Brining is a technique that produces well-seasoned, moist poultry, pork, or even seafood. Even though this recipe calls for brining skinless drumsticks and thighs, the meat will still be moist and tender because when roasting most meats lose 30 percent moisture—but when you brine, only 15 percent.

The crumb coating for these oven-fried chicken legs contains dried herbs. Fresh herbs are normally preferred, but in this case we do prefer dried herbs. Fresh herbs would char and burn in the high heat of the oven. Remember when using dried herbs to work them a little in the palms of your hands to make them finer. The dried herbs will then blend nicely into the crumb mixture, and there won't be any sharp stems or leaves.

1¼	cups kosher salt	4	cups panko (Japanese breadcrumbs) or dry breadcrumbs
¼	cup sugar		
2	tablespoons paprika	¼	cup canola or vegetable oil
2	medium heads garlic, finely chopped	2	large eggs, lightly beaten
4	bay leaves	2	tablespoons Dijon mustard
7	cups buttermilk	1	teaspoon dried thyme
4	whole chicken legs (4 drumsticks and 4 thighs, skin removed)	1	teaspoon dried oregano
			Coarse salt and freshly ground black pepper

- In a large plastic, sealable container combine the kosher salt, sugar, paprika, garlic, and bay leaves. Add the buttermilk and stir until the salt is completely dissolved. Immerse the chicken in the mixture and refrigerate to marinate 2 to 3 hours. Remove the chicken from the buttermilk brine and shake off the excess. Place the chicken in a single layer on a large wire rack set over a rimmed baking sheet.

- Adjust the oven rack to the upper third of the oven and preheat to 400°F. Line a sheet pan with foil and set a wire rack over the lined sheet pan. (The rack will allow the air to circulate and the chicken will cook more crisply.)

- Place the breadcrumbs in a shallow dish. Drizzle the oil over the crumbs, tossing to combine. In a second shallow dish combine the eggs, mustard, thyme, and oregano. Season with the salt and pepper to taste.

- Working one piece at a time, coat each chicken piece on both sides with the egg mixture. Place the chicken in the crumbs and press to coat. Gently shake off the excess and place on the prepared rack. Transfer to the oven and bake until the chicken is golden brown and juices run clear when pierced with a knife, about 40 minutes. Serve immediately.

ASIAN-INSPIRED BROILED QUAIL

Makes 4 servings

Quail are also known in the South as bobwhite. The meat is white and very delicately flavored. Wild quail will taste stronger and a bit gamier than farm-raised quail. This recipe can be easily multiplied for game dinner parties.

It's easy to make a quick quail stock (say that three times fast) with the trimmed bones. Place the bones in a small saucepan with half an onion, carrot, and a stalk of celery, all coarsely chopped. Maybe add a stem or so of cilantro or a couple of trimmings of ginger peel to mirror the flavors in the marinade. Cover with water and bring to a boil. Reduce the heat to simmer and cook until fragrant and flavorful, about thirty minutes. Use this stock to deglaze the pan in the end instead of water.

6	whole jumbo quail, about 8 ounces each
½	cup packed chopped fresh cilantro leaves
2	tablespoons finely chopped peeled fresh ginger
2	garlic cloves, finely chopped
2	tablespoons soy sauce
2	teaspoons ground cumin
2	teaspoons ground coriander
2	tablespoons canola or vegetable oil
2	tablespoons sesame oil
	Coarse salt and freshly ground black pepper
3	tablespoons water or quail stock (see note above)
2	teaspoons sesame seeds, toasted

(continued)

- Using poultry shears or a sharp knife, remove the neck and first two wing joints of the quail and discard. Remove the backbone and halve lengthwise through the breast. Repeat with the remaining quail. Place the quail halves in a single layer in a shallow broiler-proof baking dish.

- Combine the chopped cilantro, ginger, garlic, soy sauce, cumin, coriander, canola, and sesame oil in a bowl. Pour the marinade over the quail, turning to coat and rubbing the marinade into both sides. Cover and refrigerate at least 1 hour and up to overnight.

- Place the oven rack 3 to 4 inches from the heat source. Preheat the oven to broil. Season the quail lightly on both sides with the salt and pepper, and arrange, skin side up, in the broiler-proof baking dish with the marinade. Transfer to the oven and cook until the skin is crisped, about 6 minutes. Turn the quail over, baste with the pan juices, and continue to broil until the desired temperature, about 3 minutes for medium doneness.

- Transfer the quail to a serving platter and tent loosely with foil to keep warm. Skim the fat from the pan juices. Place the pan on the stovetop over medium-high heat. Add the 3 tablespoons water and stir with a wooden spoon to scrape up any browned bits. Taste and adjust for seasoning with salt and pepper. Spoon the pan juices over the quail, sprinkle with the sesame seeds, and serve immediately.

CRISPY DUCK BREASTS WITH PORT-CHERRY REDUCTION

Makes 4 servings

Duck is a dark poultry with rich, meaty flesh that marries very nicely with fruity flavors such as cherry or orange. The skin is quite thick and fatty, and needs to be scored so that it will render the fat and the skin will brown and crisp.

The sauce is made with port, a rich, fruity wine that complements the duck. Port is a sweet, fortified wine most often served after a meal as a digestive or digestif. Port originated in Portugal, although it is now produced in other countries as well. There are many different types of port and it can be confusing. The most expensive are known as vintage ports. These are made from grapes of a single vintage, bottled within two years, and aged fifty years or more. These are not for cooking. Tawny ports are a blend of grapes from several years, then aged in wood, and ready to drink when bottled. Ruby ports are the lowest grade of port, least expensive, and also ready to drink when bottled. They are the lightest and fruitiest in flavor and best for cooking.

1	cup soy sauce
1	cup sherry
4	(6-ounce) duck breast halves
12	cherries, pitted and halved, thawed if frozen
2	cups homemade chicken stock or reduced-fat, low-sodium chicken broth
½	cup port
1	fresh thyme sprig
1	teaspoon cornstarch
2	teaspoons water
2	tablespoons unsalted butter, cut into ½-inch pieces
	Coarse salt and freshly ground black pepper

(continued)

- Combine the soy sauce and sherry in a medium bowl.

- Using a sharp knife, score the duck breasts skin (not through the meat) in diagonal cuts at $\frac{1}{2}$-inch intervals. Place the ducks, skin side up, in a glass baking dish. Pour the marinade over the ducks, cover with plastic wrap, and refrigerate at least 2 and up to 4 hours.

- Bring the cherries, chicken stock, port, and thyme sprig to a boil in a medium saucepan over high heat. Simmer until the mixture is reduced to $\frac{1}{2}$ cup, about 15 minutes.

- Meanwhile, heat a heavy, large skillet over high heat. Remove the duck breasts from the marinade. Discard the marinade. Without crowding, add the duck breasts, skin side down, to the skillet. (You may need to do this in two batches.) Cook until the skin is crispy, about 10 minutes. Turn the ducks over and continue cooking to desired doneness, about 5 minutes for medium. Transfer the ducks to a clean cutting board to rest.

- Combine the cornstarch and water in a small cup to make a slurry. Add the cornstarch mixture to the port-cherry reduction. Bring the mixture to a simmer, whisking constantly. Add the butter a little at a time, whisking until the butter is combined before adding the next piece. Taste and adjust for seasoning with salt and pepper. Slice the duck breasts thinly on the diagonal and fan out on serving plates. Spoon the port-cherry sauce over and serve immediately.

BEEF, LAMB
& GAME

Often when we have a special occasion we celebrate with a fine meal at home or by dining out. A thick, juicy steak or a crusty lamb chop is often what's on the plate. I've included some recipes that will help you dazzle you dinner guests. But it's not all fancy; I've got Oven-Braised Brisket & Onions and Sunday Pot Roast. There's a little something for everyone and every occasion. If you live in an area where fresh game is not a rarity and like cooking game, here are few new recipes for your recipe box. If not, many of the cuts called for are available in gourmet markets or online. One way or the other, you will really enjoy the recipes in this chapter.

OVEN-BRAISED BRISKET & ONIONS

Makes 8 to 10 servings

This is a simple, old-fashioned recipe that is certain to become a family favorite. And you essentially put a bunch of really great ingredients in a pot and walk away for three hours. What's even better is that this dish gets even tastier after a day or so.

Brisket is a cut of beef taken from the breast section. It is a tough piece of meat, but with long, slow cooking, it becomes delicious. Brisket is divided into two sections. The flat cut has less fat and is usually more expensive than the more flavorful point cut, which has more fat. (Fat equals flavor—you make the call.) Corned beef is made from brisket, so make certain to tell your butcher you want fresh, not corned, brisket.

2	plus 2 tablespoons canola oil
1	(5 to 6-pound) piece beef brisket (not corned beef)
	Coarse salt and freshly ground black pepper
3	large yellow onions, cut into ½-inch slices
4	garlic cloves, finely chopped
2	teaspoons paprika, preferably Hungarian
2	bay leaves
3	cups beef stock or reduced-fat, low-sodium beef broth, more if needed

- Preheat the oven to 375°F. Heat 2 tablespoons canola oil in a large Dutch oven over medium-high heat. Pat the brisket dry and season with salt and pepper to taste. Sear the brisket on both sides 8 to 10 minutes. (A good dark brown sear is important and equals flavor.) Transfer the meat from the pot to a plate.

- Add the remaining 2 tablespoons oil to the Dutch oven over medium-high heat. Add the onions and cook, stirring, until softened and beginning to turn golden, 5 to 7 minutes. Add the garlic, paprika, and salt and pepper to taste, and cook until fragrant, 45 to 60 seconds. Add the bay leaves and beef broth, and bring to a boil.

- Return the seared brisket to the Dutch oven, leaving the lid ½ inch ajar. Transfer to the oven and bake until tender, about 3½ hours. Add more water or stock as needed throughout the roasting time.

- Remove the pot from the oven. Transfer the brisket to a cutting board. Remove and discard the bay leaves. Using a handheld blender, purée the onions to smooth. Taste and adjust for seasoning with the salt and pepper. Slice the brisket against the grain and serve with the onion purée.

SUNDAY POT ROAST

Makes 4 to 6 servings

Sunday suppers mean sitting at the table with family and friends with good food and fellowship. A pot roast is an excellent recipe for Sunday supper. Everybody should have a great pot roast recipe and here is the one. The meat is moist, tender, and cooked with a special combination of herbs and spices.

It's all about choosing the cut of meat. This recipe calls for rump roast and the name says it all. It comes from the rump of the cow. It is the most tender as well as the most flavorful cut from the round, which is the hindquarter of the steer from the ankles to the rump. The hindquarters are toughened by exercise, so they are more flavorful, but also need long, slow cooking.

3	tablespoons olive oil		2	cups beef stock or reduced-fat, low-sodium beef broth, more if needed
1	(4-pound) boneless rump roast			
3	medium onions, sliced		1	cup dry red wine
2	tablespoons paprika, preferably Hungarian		1	cup water
2	bay leaves		2	pounds new potatoes, scrubbed
1	teaspoon dried rosemary		8	carrots, cut into 1½-inch-thick pieces
1	teaspoon dried oregano			
1	teaspoon dried thyme			Coarse salt and freshly ground black pepper
4	garlic cloves, crushed			

- Preheat the oven to 300°F. Heat the oil in a large, heavy-bottom Dutch oven over medium-high heat. Add the roast and sear on all sides, 8 to 10 minutes. (A good dark brown sear is important and equals flavor.)

- Transfer the roast from the pot to a plate. Reduce the heat to medium. Add the onions and cook, stirring frequently, until deep golden brown, 8 to 10 minutes. Add the paprika, bay leaves, rosemary, oregano, thyme, and garlic. Stir to combine and cook until fragrant, 45 to 60 seconds.

- Add the broth, wine, and water. Bring to a boil. Add the potatoes and carrots. Return the roast plus any accumulated juices to the Dutch oven. Season with the salt and pepper to taste. Cover with a tight-fitting lid.

- Transfer to the oven and bake for 2 hours. Turn the roast, add stock if necessary, cover, and bake an additional hour or until tender. Remove the pot from the oven. Transfer the roast to a warm platter. Tent loosely with foil to keep it warm. Remove and discard the bay leaves. Taste the sauce and adjust the seasoning with more salt and pepper if necessary. Spoon the sauce and vegetables over the roast and serve immediately.

OLD-FASHIONED MEATLOAF

Makes 4 servings

Everybody loves meatloaf. It's one of those dishes you grew up eating. It's comfort food. Nowadays it is often associated with blue-plate specials in diners and truck stops. Made at home, it takes on a whole new feeling. Served with a side of buttery mashed potatoes, you simply cannot get much better than this. (Except for a meatloaf sandwich the next day.)

Like most down-home recipes, this one is subject to considerable variation, from your choice of meats to the specific selection of seasonings. A combination of beef, pork, and veal is best for maximum flavor and tenderness. The oatmeal helps bind the meat and absorbs the cooking juices, resulting in a moist, tender loaf. Be careful not to overknead the meatloaf ingredients; doing so will make your meatloaf heavy and dense.

1	pound lean ground beef
¼	pound ground pork
¼	pound ground veal
2	large eggs, lightly beaten
¾	cup milk
½	cup oatmeal
½	cup canned peeled tomatoes, drained and roughly chopped
2	celery stalks, finely diced
1	medium onion, finely diced
1	garlic clove, finely chopped
1	tablespoon dried basil
1	tablespoon dried thyme
1	tablespoon dried oregano
	Coarse salt and freshly ground black pepper

- Preheat the oven to 425°F. Oil a 13 x 9 x 2-inch loaf pan.
- Using a large bowl, combine the beef, pork, and veal. In a separate medium bowl combine the beaten eggs, milk, and oatmeal. Pour the egg mixture into the meat mixture and use your hands to combine. Add the tomatoes, celery, onion, garlic, basil, thyme, and oregano. Season with the salt and pepper to taste and combine thoroughly. Form into a loaf and place in a loaf pan. Transfer to the oven and bake until cooked through, about 45 minutes. Remove to a rack to cool slightly. Slice and serve immediately.

BRAISED SHORT RIBS WITH DIJON MUSTARD

Makes 4 servings

Braising is a classic cooking technique by which meat or vegetables are first browned in fat, then cooked, tightly covered, in a small amount of liquid over low heat for a long time. Cooking food slowly for a long time is what develops flavor and tenderizes it by gently breaking down the fibers. Slow cooking is good cooking.

Short ribs, also known as flanken, are rectangles of beef about 2 inches by 3 inches, usually taken from the chuck. They consist of layers of fat and meat and contain pieces of the rib bone. They're very tough and require long, slow, moist-heat cooking.

4	cups dry red wine
4	pounds beef short ribs
	Coarse salt and freshly ground black pepper
2	tablespoons canola oil
12	medium shallots, peeled
½	cup whole-grain Dijon mustard
8	plum tomatoes, halved lengthwise

- Using a 2-quart, heavy-bottom saucepan over high heat, bring the wine to a boil and reduce to about 1 cup.

- Meanwhile, pat the ribs dry and season generously with salt and pepper.

- Heat the oil in a heavy-bottom Dutch oven over medium-high heat until smoking. Add the ribs in three batches to brown on all sides, about 8 minutes for each batch. Remove the ribs to a plate.

- Reduce the heat to medium and sauté shallots in the rendered fat remaining in the pot, stirring until browned. Add the wine reduction, mustard, and tomatoes to the pot and stir to combine. Return the ribs and any accumulated juices. Season with the salt and pepper. Bring to a boil and then reduce the heat to simmer. Cover and simmer the ribs until tender, 2 to 2½ hours.

- Carefully transfer ribs, shallots, and tomatoes to a serving platter. Tent loosely with aluminum foil to keep warm. Skim off any fat from the cooking liquid. Return to the heat and reduce until slightly thickened. Taste and adjust for seasoning with salt and pepper. Pour over the ribs and serve immediately.

Marvin at the Memphis in May BBQ festival.

BEEF TENDERLOIN
WITH BALSAMIC PORT REDUCTION

Makes 4 servings

Beef tenderloin is the least used muscle on the cow so it is extremely tender. It's so tender you can cut it with a fork. This is a deluxe, very expensive cut of beef. The tenderloin can be roasted whole or cut into smaller roasts and steaks.

The steaks are complemented with a sweet and sour balsamic port reduction. The pan sauce utilizes a classic French technique known as mounting. To mount a sauce means to whisk cold chunks of butter into a sauce off the heat just before serving to improve the flavor and give it a silky smooth appearance. Serve these steaks with the Grits with Fontina and Bacon (page 121) and steamed asparagus for a memorable, elegant meal.

2	cups port
2	cups dry white wine
4	(6-ounce) beef tenderloin steaks
	Coarse salt and freshly ground black pepper
	All-purpose flour for dusting
4	tablespoons (½ stick) unsalted butter, chilled and cut into pieces
2	tablespoons olive oil
¼	cup balsamic vinegar

- Heat the port and white wine in a small, heavy-bottom saucepan over high heat. Reduce to about 1⅓ cups, about 8 minutes.

- Season the steaks on both sides with salt and pepper. Dust lightly with flour and shake to remove excess flour. (The steaks should be very lightly dusted.)

- Heat 2 tablespoons butter and 2 tablespoons oil in a large, heavy-bottom sauté pan over medium-high heat. Add the steaks and cook to desired doneness, about 4 minutes per side for medium-rare. Transfer the steaks to a platter. Tent loosely with aluminum foil to keep warm.

- Add the port reduction and vinegar to the sauté pan over high heat and bring to a boil, scraping up any browned bits. Boil until slightly thickened, about 2 minutes. Remove from the heat. Add the remaining butter, one piece at a time, swirling the pan until the butter is just melted. Taste and adjust for seasoning with salt and pepper. Spoon the sauce over the steaks and serve immediately.

DROPPIN' KNOWLEDGE

Beef tenderloin is the most tender cut, but rib-eye steaks are the most flavorful. Rib-eye steaks are very well marbled which results in a buttery tenderness and great taste. Marbling is an even distribution of fat throughout the meat, and fat means flavor.

PECAN LAMB LOIN CHOPS

Makes 4 servings

Lamb is produced from animals less than a year old. There's no real need to buy "spring lamb." In earlier times this indicated a lamb born in February or March, fed on milk in the spring, and butchered in the fall. These lambs were young, tender, and highly sought after. Now that term has little meaning other than as a marketing tool.

Loin lamb chops are cut from the loin and look more like a miniature T-bone steak with a bit on the loin and tenderloin on either side. The meat is earthy, rich, and faintly sweet. The light, crispy coating of fragrant rosemary and toasted pecans is an excellent complement.

1	cup pecan halves
2	sprigs fresh rosemary
	Coarse salt and freshly ground black pepper
2	large egg whites, lightly beaten
½	cup all-purpose flour
8	(6-ounce) lamb loin chops, about 1½ inches thick
2	plus 2 tablespoons vegetable oil

- In the bowl of a food processor fitted with a blade attachment, process the pecans and rosemary until finely chopped. Spread on a large plate and season with salt and pepper.

- Whisk the egg whites in a medium bowl until light and frothy. Place the flour in a shallow bowl and season generously with the salt and pepper. Dredge the lamb chops in the flour mixture to coat, shaking off the excess flour. Dip the flour-coated chops in the egg whites and finally into the ground pecans, coating all sides.

- Heat 2 tablespoons oil in a large, nonstick sauté pan over medium-high heat. Add the chops, in batches if necessary, and cook until brown on both sides, 4 to 5 minutes per side for rare. (Add the remaining 2 tablespoons oil for the second batch.) Serve immediately.

[SEE PHOTO ON PAGE 168]

ROSEMARY & GARLIC LAMB CHOPS

Makes 4 servings

Lamb rib chops are cut from a rack of lamb. They usually contain one rib per chop, but you'll get a thicker and juicier steak with a double-cut lamb rib chop, which includes two ribs. Lamb rib chops are normally "frenched" by removing 1½ inches of meat from the bone ends and exposing the bone. This makes for a nice presentation, a little "handle" for the chop.

Rosemary and mint are two herbs that are natural partners to the rich taste of lamb. The herb rosemary has slender, slightly curved leaves that resemble miniature curved pine needles. Rosemary is found in bouquet garni, Herbes de Provence, and seasoning blends for lamb and Mediterranean cuisines. Mint has dark green leaves and has a pleasant, aromatic, sweet flavor with a cool aftertaste. Both herbs are best used fresh and not dried.

6	garlic cloves
4	tablespoons extra-virgin olive oil
1	tablespoon chopped fresh rosemary
1	tablespoon chopped fresh mint
8	lamb rib chops, about 2½ ounces each
	Coarse salt and freshly ground black pepper

- Place the oven rack 4 to 5 inches from the heat source. Preheat the oven to broil.

- In the bowl of the food processor fitted with a blade attachment, process the garlic, oil, rosemary, and mint. Season the chops with salt and pepper. Rub the chops on both sides with the garlic mixture.

- Arrange the chops in a single layer on a baking sheet. Transfer to the oven and broil the chops until cooked to desired doneness, 3 to 4 minutes per side for medium-rare. Serve immediately.

PAN-SEARED VENISON
WITH ROSEMARY & DRIED CHERRIES

Makes 8 servings

Venison is a broad term that refers to meat from a variety of game animals such as deer, elk, moose, caribou, and antelope. The nutritional value and the quality of venison depend on the type of animal, age of the animal, diet, and if wild, the time of year hunted. In spring, for example, after a long winter and scarce food, the meat is tougher and leaner. In general, game meat is leaner than meat from domesticated animals.

Since moose and antelope are few and far between in the South, this recipe uses deer. Domesticated deer meat is available in specialty or gourmet grocery stores and online.

1	tablespoon chopped fresh rosemary	½	cup dry red wine
2	teaspoons coriander seeds	½	cup dried tart cherries
3	garlic cloves, chopped	1½	cups beef stock or reduced-fat, low-sodium beef broth
1	plus 1 tablespoon olive oil	1	cup water
2	venison tenderloins, about 1 pound each	2	teaspoons cornstarch
	Coarse salt and freshly ground black pepper	2	tablespoons honey

- Preheat the oven to 450°F. In an electric spice grinder combine the rosemary, coriander seeds, and garlic to make a paste. Add 1 teaspoon olive oil and pulse to combine.

- Pat the venison dry with a paper towel. Divide the paste in half and rub each tenderloin evenly with the paste. Cover and refrigerate to marinate for 20 minutes.

- Heat the remaining olive oil in a heavy-bottom, ovenproof skillet over high heat. Season the venison with salt and pepper. Cook the tenderloins until browned, turning once, about 6 minutes.

- Transfer the skillet to the oven and roast until an instant-read thermometer inserted diagonally into the center registers 125°F, 8 to 10 minutes. Transfer the meat to a plate and tent loosely with aluminum foil. Add the wine and cherries to the skillet over medium-high heat, stirring with a wooden spoon to loosen any browned bits in the pan.

- In a small bowl combine the beef stock, water, and cornstarch. Whisk into the wine mixture and simmer until thickened, about 5 minutes. Whisk in the honey. Taste and adjust for seasoning with salt and pepper. Thinly slice the venison and serve immediately with the sauce.

FISH & SEAFOOD

Seafood can be a bit intimidating. How long do I cook the fish? What do I season it with? What do I serve with it? Well, you'll find some answers to those questions in this chapter. Unless the piece of fish is bigger than a typical six- to eight-ounce serving, or contains a bone, you are probably looking at five to seven minutes cooking time maximum. How's that for quick and easy? Even the busiest executive has seven minutes to spare for a healthy, full-flavored seafood dish. When purchasing seafood, if the fish is whole, the eyes should be clear. The fish shouldn't smell fishy, and the flesh shouldn't be soft to the touch; it should have some firmness to it.

Fish is one of the healthiest meats, be brave and creative with the following recipes.

CRAB-STUFFED FLOUNDER

Makes 6 servings

There are many varieties of flounder around the world. Flounder are bottom-dwelling flatfish with both eyes on one side. They can be purchased either whole or as fillets. The flesh is mild and delicate with a flaky, tender texture. Flounder can be cooked in numerous ways, including poaching, broiling, sautéing, and baking. Flounder is low in fat and because of this, overcooking tends to dry the fish out. (No problem here because we're adding lots of butter.)

Crab stuffing should be crab, not breadcrumbs. Buy the best-quality crab and don't overwork it so the lumps of crab stay whole. This is an old-time, rich, buttery dish, reminiscent of seafood shacks on the Gulf of Mexico.

4	plus 2 plus 2 tablespoons (1 stick) unsalted butter
1	celery stalk, finely chopped
1	small onion, finely chopped
¼	cup chopped fresh parsley
5	ounces jumbo lump crabmeat, picked through for any shells or cartilage
½	cup panko (Japanese breadcrumbs) or dry breadcrumbs
1	tablespoon lemon juice
	Coarse salt and freshly ground pepper
6	flounder fillets
¼	teaspoon paprika
	Lemon wedges for garnish

- Preheat the oven to 400°F. Coat the bottom of a 9 x 13-inch baking dish with 2 tablespoons butter.

- Melt 4 tablespoons butter in a large skillet over medium heat. Add the celery and onion and cook until the vegetables are tender, about 5 minutes. Remove from the heat and transfer to a bowl to cool slightly. Add the parsley, crabmeat, breadcrumbs, and lemon juice. Stir to combine. Taste and adjust for seasoning with the salt and pepper.

- Divide the crabmeat mixture evenly over the fillets. Starting at the narrow end, roll each fillet jelly-roll-style and secure with a toothpick. Place the rolls seam side down in the baking dish.

- Melt the remaining 2 tablespoons butter and drizzle over the fillets. Sprinkle the tops with the paprika. Transfer the fillets to the oven and bake until the fish flakes and is cooked through, 18 to 20 minutes. Garnish with lemon wedges and serve immediately.

NEW ORLEANS BARBECUED SHRIMP

Makes 8 to 10 appetizer portions

When buying shrimp, ask to smell them. They should smell like the ocean or nothing—and particularly not like ammonia. Few rules govern the sale of shrimp and size classifications vary store to store. Learn to judge shrimp as chefs do— by the number of shrimp it takes to make a pound. Large typically means fifteen to twenty per pound and is the best combination of flavor and value.

The biggest mistake in cooking shrimp is cooking them too long. Most people overcook them, and the shrimp taste like rubber. Shrimp should only take two to three minutes to cook. Normally, it's best to use fresh herbs, but this take on barbecued shrimp is a Big Easy classic. If it's not broke, don't fix it. These shrimp are served with a crusty baguette to sop up all the delicious juices. This appetizer is so simple—you're going to love it.

1	cup (2 sticks) unsalted butter
½	cup olive oil
4	garlic cloves, finely chopped
4	whole bay leaves, finely crushed
2	teaspoons finely crushed dried rosemary leaves
½	teaspoon dried basil
½	teaspoon dried oregano
½	teaspoon dried thyme
½	teaspoon red pepper flakes
1	tablespoon paprika
	Juice of ½ lemon
2	pounds large shrimp, head on, in the shell
	Coarse salt and freshly ground black pepper
	Crusty baguette for serving

- Combine the butter and oil in a heavy-bottom, ovenproof saucepan over medium heat. Add the garlic, bay leaves, rosemary, basil, oregano, thyme, salt to taste, red pepper, paprika, and lemon juice. Cook, stirring constantly, until the sauce begins to boil. Reduce the heat to low, and simmer, stirring frequently, until the flavors have infused, 7 to 8 minutes.

- Add the shrimp and toss to coat. Cook the shrimp, stirring, over medium heat just until the shrimp turn pink, 3 to 4 minutes. Taste and adjust for seasoning with the salt and pepper. Serve immediately with the crusty baguette.

[SEE PHOTO ON PAGE 180]

Makes 4 servings

Étoufée is a succulent, tangy, tomato stew usually made with crawfish or shrimp. The preparation traditionally starts with a dark brown roux. Crawfish and shrimp étoufées are New Orleans and Cajun-country specialties. The word comes from the French *étouffer*, which means "to smother" or "to suffocate." This recipe uses cornstarch instead of a roux as a shortcut, so you can have étoufée in thirty minutes or fewer.

Crawfish are also known as mudbugs, crawdads, or crayfish. These freshwater crustaceans, in season from December to May, range in size from three to six inches and weigh from two to eight ounces. In some parts of the South they are considered bait, but don't say that to a Cajun. Crawfish are available cooked in the shell and shelled in larger grocery stores, or fresh by mail order from several Louisiana sources.

4	tablespoons (½ stick) unsalted butter	1	pound shelled crawfish tails
1	small white onion, diced	2	tablespoons chopped fresh parsley
1	celery stalk, diced	¼	teaspoon cayenne
1	small green bell pepper, seeded and diced		Coarse salt and freshly ground black pepper
3	garlic cloves, finely chopped		Hot cooked rice
1	tablespoon tomato paste	2	scallions, chopped
1	teaspoon cornstarch		
¾	cup homemade chicken stock or reduced-fat, low-sodium chicken broth		

- Heat the butter in a large sauté pan over medium-high heat. Add the onion, celery, bell pepper, and garlic. Cook until tender, stirring frequently, 8 to 10 minutes. Add the tomato paste and stir to combine.

- In a small bowl, combine the cornstarch and stock. Add the stock mixture to the sauté pan and bring to a boil, stirring constantly.

- Add the crawfish, parsley, and cayenne. Cook until heated through, about 5 minutes. Taste and adjust for seasoning with salt and pepper. Spoon over the hot rice. Garnish with the scallions and serve immediately.

GULF COAST OYSTER PO' BOYS

Makes 4 servings

The myth about buying oysters only in the months with an "R" is just that, a myth. However, it is best to buy oysters during the fall and winter when they are at their best. Oysters spawn during the summer months and become soft and fatty. Shuck 'em if you wish, but you can generally find pints of shucked oysters in better grocery stores and markets.

Peanut oil is a great oil for frying, because it has a pleasant flavor, does not take on tastes from foods as readily as other oils, and has a smoke point of about 450°F—this means it takes very high temperatures to cause it to burn. Asian peanut oil, however, is completely different. It has the fragrance of freshly roasted peanuts and is not good for frying.

½	cup mayonnaise		1½	cups yellow cornmeal
2	teaspoons hot sauce		2	cups shucked oysters, about 3 dozen, drained
	Juice of ½ lemon			
	Coarse salt and freshly ground black pepper		1	loaf soft-crusted bread, about 14 inches long, cut in half horizontally
6	cups peanut oil for frying			
1	large egg, lightly beaten		3	cups shredded iceberg lettuce
¼	cup milk		1	large ripe tomato, sliced
1	plus 1½ teaspoons salt			

- In a small bowl combine the mayonnaise, hot sauce, and lemon juice. Season with the salt and pepper to taste. Heat the oil in a deep, heavy pot over high heat until it registers 375°F.

- Meanwhile, combine the egg, milk, and 1 teaspoon salt in a bowl. Combine the cornmeal, the remaining 1½ teaspoons salt, and pepper to taste in a sealable, plastic bag.

- Working in batches, add the oysters to the egg mixture. Then lift out the oysters, letting the excess egg mixture drip off. Put the oysters in the cornmeal mixture, shaking to coat well.

- Carefully put the oysters in the oil and fry, turning occasionally, until golden and just cooked through, 1 to 2 minutes. Using a slotted spoon, transfer the oysters to a plate lined with paper towels to drain. Taste and adjust for seasoning with salt and pepper. Repeat the process, returning oil to 375°F for each batch.

- Spread the mayonnaise on both pieces of bread. Sandwich the oysters, lettuce, and tomato slices between the bread. Cut into four pieces and serve immediately.

LIGHTENED SHRIMP PO' BOYS

Makes 4 servings

Po' boys are a large sandwich made with French bread that began as a five-cent lunch for poor boys. Po' boys are typically filled with fried oysters, shrimp, fish, and crawfish. They are also known as peacemakers. Legend has it that in the nineteenth century, a New Orleans husband who had spent the night in the saloons of the French Quarter brought this oyster sandwich home to his wife as a "peacemaker." Regardless of the origin or even the name, you are guaranteed to like this sandwich.

This version is lighter and healthier than the deep-fried versions. The shrimp are breaded in egg whites and coated in panko, or Japanese breadcrumbs. Panko gives food a lighter and crunchier texture than any other breadcrumbs. You can find them at Asian markets and most gourmet stores.

2	large egg whites	2	cups shredded iceberg lettuce
1	tablespoon water	2	tablespoons low-fat tartar sauce
	Coarse salt and freshly ground black pepper	1	teaspoon hot sauce (or to taste)
½	cup panko (Japanese breadcrumbs)	1	large tomato, very thinly sliced
16	large shrimp, peeled, deveined, and butterflied	4	(2½-ounce) hoagie rolls with sesame seeds, split
2	tablespoons canola or olive oil	1	lemon, quartered

- Combine the egg whites and water in a small bowl and whisk until light and frothy. Season with the salt and pepper. Place the breadcrumbs in another shallow dish. Dredge the shrimp in the egg-white mixture and then dredge them in the breadcrumbs.

- Heat the oil in a large, nonstick skillet over medium-high heat. Add the breaded shrimp without overcrowding the skillet. Cook 2 to 3 minutes per side until golden brown. If your skillet is not large enough, you may need to cook the shrimp in two batches, and you may need to add a little more oil.

- Combine the lettuce, tartar sauce, and hot sauce in a medium bowl. Season with salt and pepper to taste.

- Arrange 3 tomato slices over the bottom half of each roll. Top each with 4 shrimp, ½ cup lettuce mixture, and the top halves of the rolls. Garnish with lemon wedges and serve immediately.

CAJUN CATFISH TENDERS WITH SPICY TARTAR SAUCE

Makes 4 servings

Catfish are bottom dwellers, so if wild, they pick up a distinctive earthy flavor. Today most catfish are farm-raised, which means they are bred in clear water and fed grain pellets. This results in a sweeter and cleaner fish flavor. When frying, make sure not to crowd the pot or the tenders will be soggy and greasy.

These tenders get a kick from Cajun seasoning. This is a motley blend of pepper, garlic powder, onion powder, allspice, nutmeg, cayenne, and salt—depending on the chef. Make certain if you buy a prepared version that salt is not the first ingredient.

DROPPIN' KNOWLEDGE

The smoke point is the temperature at which fat begins to break down, burn, and smoke. The higher the smoke point, the better suited it is for high heat and frying. The more refined an oil is, the higher the smoke point.

- Extra-virgin olive oil—250°F
- Butter—350°F
- Refined canola oil—400°F
- Olive oil—410°F
- Refined peanut oil—450°F

FOR THE TARTAR SAUCE:

1	cup mayonnaise
1/4	cup sweet pickle relish
3	tablespoons capers, rinsed, drained, and chopped
	Grated zest of half a lemon
1	tablespoon fresh lemon juice
2	teaspoons prepared horseradish
1	tablespoon hot sauce
2	teaspoons Cajun seasoning

FOR THE CATFISH:

1	large egg
2	tablespoons milk
1	tablespoon hot sauce
1¼	pounds catfish fillets, cut diagonally into ½-inch-wide strips
2	quarts peanut oil, plus more if needed
½	cup all-purpose flour
½	cup fine yellow cornmeal
3	teaspoons Cajun seasoning
	Coarse salt and freshly ground black pepper
	Lemon wedges (optional)

- For the tartar sauce, combine in a small bowl the mayonnaise, relish, capers, lemon zest, lemon juice, horseradish, hot sauce, and Cajun seasoning.
- For the catfish, whisk together the egg, milk, and hot sauce in a large shallow dish.
- Add the fish strips and marinate at room temperature for 15 minutes. Pour enough peanut oil into a 4-quart, heavy-bottom pot to measure 2 inches. Heat the oil over medium-high heat until a thermometer registers 350°F.

Executive Producer Mike Thomas droppin' a little knowledge on Marvin in Birmingham, Alabama.

CAJUN CATFISH TENDERS WITH SPICY TARTAR SAUCE

(continued)

- Combine the flour, cornmeal, Cajun seasoning, and salt and pepper to taste in a second shallow dish. Remove about one-quarter of the fish, allowing the excess egg to drip off. Dredge the fish in the flour mixture, shaking off the excess. Transfer the fish to the oil and fry, stirring occasionally, until golden and just cooked through, about 2 minutes.

- Using a slotted spoon, transfer the fish to paper towels to drain. Allow the oil temperature to return to 350°F. Repeat the procedure with the remaining fish in batches. Serve with lemon wedges, if desired.

TROUT WITH LEMONS & CAPERS

Makes 2 to 4 servings

Trout is a popular cold water, freshwater fish. In the South, the lower Appalachian Mountains provide an excellent habitat for wild trout. Farm-raised trout is also widely available. Be careful; trout has a mild delicate flavor and overcooks easily. A short cooking time not only keeps the fish moist and tender, but also helps accommodate busy schedules.

This is a version of a classic French dish known as Trout Grenobloise. Grenobloise means that the fish is sautéed in butter and garnished with lemon and capers. Capers are the pickled flower buds of a Mediterranean shrub. They have a sharp, distinctive flavor. Capers are packed in brine, salt, or vinegar, so it is best to rinse them before using.

½   cup all-purpose flour

1   teaspoon coarse salt, plus additional

½   teaspoon freshly ground black pepper, plus additional

2   (12-ounce) trout, butterflied

2   tablespoons canola oil

1   tablespoon unsalted butter

     Juice of 1 lemon

1   tablespoon capers, rinsed

¼   cup chopped fresh parsley

- Place the flour in a shallow dish. Add 1 teaspoon salt and ½ teaspoon black pepper, and stir with a fork to combine. Season the butterflied trout lightly with more salt and pepper. Pat both sides of the trout in flour, shaking gently to remove the excess flour.

- Heat the oil in a large skillet over medium-high heat. Add the trout to the skillet, skin side up. Cook until pale golden, about 3 minutes. Turn and continue cooking, 3 to 4 minutes more.

- Remove the trout to a warmed serving platter. Remove the skillet from the heat. Add the butter, lemon juice, and capers. Brown the butter, stirring with a wooden spoon to release the brown bits in the bottom of the skillet, 1 to 2 minutes. Add the parsley and swirl to combine. Pour the sauce over trout and serve immediately.

HONEY & DIJON MUSTARD SALMON

Makes 6 servings

Home cooks are generally timid when it comes to cooking fish. Salmon is becoming the exception. Salmon is widely available in steaks as well as fillets. Farm-raised salmon is available year-round. The flesh is firm and oily, and does not dry out easily. Salmon is an excellent source of protein, a rich source of vitamin A, the B-group vitamins, and omega-3 oils. (Omega-3 oils are good for your heart and cholesterol levels.)

This straightforward recipe uses a few simple ingredients. Remember: The fewer the ingredients, the better the components have to be. Buy the fish from a good source. The flesh should be firm, smell fresh and clean, and the skin should have a sheen. Salmon is delicious when cooked to medium or medium-rare—the exterior is well cooked and the center is nearly raw. Give it a try.

3   tablespoons chopped fresh dill
3   tablespoons Dijon mustard
2   tablespoons honey
6   (4-ounce) salmon fillets
       Coarse salt and freshly ground black pepper

- Place the oven rack about 6 inches from the heat source. Preheat the oven to broil. In a small bowl whisk together the dill, mustard, and honey.
- Rinse the salmon fillets and pat them dry with paper towels. Season with the salt and pepper.
- Spray the broiler pan with vegetable oil. Brush the flesh side of the salmon fillets with the honey mixture. Place the fish, skin side down, on the broiler pan.
- Transfer to the oven and broil until the fish is firm, about 6 minutes for medium-rare. Serve immediately.

DROPPIN' KNOWLEDGE

To prevent contamination from bacteria, foods must be cooked to a certain temperature in order to kill the bacteria:

- Poultry and stuffed foods—165°F or greater
- Fish and ground beef—155°F
- Pork, steak, eggs, and game and exotic animals—145°F
- Fruits and vegetables—140°F
- Roast beef and corned beef—130°F

DESSERTS

Sweet tooth anyone? I'm not going to say that we saved the best for last because there are great recipes throughout this book, but if you do like dessert, then you'll definitely enjoy the following pages. Of course, we had to give you the classic southern desserts like strawberry shortcake, Mississippi mud cake, and our very own cobbler. And no cookout or family celebration is complete without a pie. With these recipes you can now compete on a level playing field with the signature dessert your favorite aunt brings to every event.

EASY PEACH COBBLER

Makes 8 servings

Cobblers come in a variety of styles and flavors. There are many opinions about which version is better—batter crust, biscuit, pastry, or crumb. This version is a batter cobbler. The batter is poured into a hot casserole with melted butter. This immediately crisps the batter and has an effect much like popovers as the batter swells.

Frozen peaches are fine and may be substituted. Other fruits include blueberry, blackberry, plum, cherry, and apricot.

½	cup (1 stick) unsalted butter
4	cups sliced peaches with juices
1	cup sugar
1	cup all-purpose flour
2	teaspoons baking powder
	Pinch of salt
1	cup milk
1	teaspoon vanilla extract
	Whipped cream, crème frâiche, or ice cream for serving

- Place the butter in a large casserole or cast-iron skillet and put it in a cold oven. Preheat the oven to 350°F. (If the peaches are not juicy and sweet, sprinkle them with some of the sugar.)

- Sift the flour, baking powder, and salt into a mixing bowl. Add the remaining sugar, milk, and vanilla extract and stir until evenly blended. When the butter has melted and the oven has reached 350°F, pour the batter all at once into the dish and add the peaches and juices to the center of the batter.

- Return the dish to the oven and bake until the top is golden brown and a cake tester poked into the batter comes out clean, about 1 hour. Serve hot, warm, or at room temperature with cream, crème frâiche, or ice cream.

QUICK & EASY FUDGE

Makes 2 pounds

Everyone needs a pantry dessert, something that can be pulled out at the last minute to satisfy the southern sweet tooth. This Quick and Easy Fudge fits the bill.

This recipe uses marshmallows and evaporated milk to help set the fudge. Marshmallows are a mixture of corn syrup or sugar, gelatin, gum Arabic, and flavoring. The texture and consistency of the marshmallow helps create a smooth, creamy fudge.

2	cups sugar
½	cup evaporated milk
½	cup (1 stick) unsalted butter, room temperature, plus more for the pan
12	large marshmallows
	Pinch of salt
1	cup (6 ounces) semisweet chocolate chips
1	cup chopped pecans
1	teaspoon pure vanilla extract

- Grease an 8-inch square pan with butter. In a heavy-duty saucepan combine the sugar, evaporated milk, butter, marshmallows, and salt. Over medium heat cook the mixture, stirring constantly. Bring to a boil and continue stirring and cooking for 5 minutes, and then remove from the heat.

- Stir the chocolate chips into the marshmallow mixture until completely melted. Add the pecans and vanilla and stir to combine. Pour the mixture into the prepared pan and allow to cool completely, about 30 minutes. Cut into squares to serve. Store in an airtight container in the refrigerator for up to two weeks.

STRAWBERRY SHORTCAKES WITH LIME & MINT

Makes 6 servings

Southern shortcakes are generally made from sweetened biscuit dough. Shortcakes from the Northeast are usually miniature sponge cakes and not biscuits at all. These are, of course, biscuit style.

Nothing beats the taste of real whipped cream. When whipping cream it is very important that the cream, bowl, and beaters be very well chilled. Don't overwhip the cream. It turns to butter.

FOR THE BISCUITS:

1¾	cups all-purpose flour, plus more for rolling
4	plus 1 tablespoons sugar
1	tablespoon baking powder
¼	teaspoon salt
¼	cup (½ stick) chilled, unsalted butter, cut into ½-inch pieces
1	cup heavy cream
1	tablespoon grated lime zest

FOR THE FILLING:

3	pints strawberries, washed, hulled, and sliced
½	cup plus 2 tablespoons sugar
2	tablespoons thinly sliced fresh mint
½	teaspoon grated lime zest
1	cup heavy cream
1	teaspoon pure vanilla extract

- Preheat the oven to 375°F. Line a baking sheet with parchment paper.

- For the biscuits, in a food processor fitted with a blade attachment, blend the flour, 4 tablespoons sugar, baking powder, and salt for 5 seconds. Add the butter and pulsate until mixture resembles coarse meal. Add the heavy cream and lime zest. Process just until mixture comes together.

- On a clean, lightly floured work surface, gather the dough into a ball. Gently knead five times. Roll out the dough to a ¾-inch thickness. Using 3-inch round cutter, cut out 6 biscuits, rerolling the dough as needed. Place the biscuits on the prepared baking sheet; sprinkle with the remaining 1 tablespoon sugar. Bake the biscuits until a light golden brown, 18 to 20 minutes. Transfer to a rack to cool.

- For the filling, place the strawberries, ½ cup sugar, mint, and lime zest in a medium bowl and stir to combine. Macerate at least 30 minutes and up to 2 hours, stirring occasionally.

- Using the bowl of an electric mixer fitted with a whisk attachment, combine the cream, vanilla, and the remaining 2 tablespoons sugar. Whisk until soft peaks form.

- To serve, cut the biscuits in half horizontally with a serrated knife. Fill with the berries and sweetened whipped cream drizzle with the remaining strawberry juice.

GEORGIA PEANUT BUTTER COOKIES

Makes about 2½ dozen cookies

The peanut is Georgia's official state crop. Georgia produces almost half of the total United States peanut crop and more than 50 percent of peanuts used in the production of peanut butter. Other peanut-producing states in the Southeast include Alabama and Florida.

All-natural peanut butter doesn't work so well as a national store brand in this recipe. These cookies are great to make with kids. Teaching kids to cook helps them learn math as well as organizational skills. But it's still good, old-fashioned fun.

½	cup peanut butter (creamy or crunchy)
½	cup unsalted butter, at room temperature
½	cup granulated sugar
½	cup firmly packed brown sugar
1	large egg
1	teaspoon pure vanilla extract
1¾	cups all-purpose flour
¾	teaspoon baking soda
½	teaspoon salt

- Preheat the oven to 375°F. In a large bowl combine the peanut butter, butter, granulated sugar, brown sugar, egg, and vanilla. In the bowl of an electric mixer fitted with the paddle attachment, beat until light and fluffy.

- In a separate bowl sift together the flour, baking soda, and salt. Stir into the butter mixture until combined. Shape the dough into 1-inch balls. Place the balls 3 inches apart on ungreased baking sheets. Gently flatten each ball with a fork in a crisscross pattern. Bake until golden brown, 8 to 10 minutes. Remove to a wire rack to cool. Store in an airtight container for up to one week.

MISSISSIPPI MUD CAKE

Makes 12 servings

Mississippi Mud Cake is a dark, rich chocolate cake topped with marshmallows, pecans, and decadent chocolate frosting. It's named after the muddy rich soil of the Mississippi River.

This cake is certain to become a family favorite. It's important to sift the confectioners' sugar and cocoa powder before making the frosting; otherwise, it's too difficult to remove the lumps.

FOR THE FROSTING:

6	tablespoons unsalted butter, room temperature
2⅔	cups confectioners' sugar, sifted
½	cup cocoa powder, sifted
⅓	cup buttermilk, plus more if needed
1	teaspoon pure vanilla extract

FOR THE CAKE:

¾	cup all-purpose flour
⅓	cup cocoa powder, sifted
½	teaspoon baking powder
½	teaspoon salt
½	cup unsalted butter, room temperature, plus more for pan
1	cup sugar
1½	teaspoons pure vanilla extract
3	large eggs
1	cup chopped pecans
1	(10-ounce) bag miniature marshmallows

- For the frosting, cream the butter in a small bowl. Add the confectioners' sugar and cocoa alternately with buttermilk. Mix to a spreading consistency, adding additional buttermilk as needed. Add the vanilla and cover.

- For the cake, preheat the oven to 350°F. Butter a 13 x 9-inch baking pan. Combine the flour, cocoa, baking powder, and salt in a small bowl.

- In the bowl of a heavy-duty mixer fitted with the paddle attachment, cream the butter, sugar, and vanilla until light and fluffy. Add the eggs, one at a time, beating well after each addition. Add the flour mixture a little at a time, scraping the sides of the bowl. Add the pecans and stir to combine. Spread the batter into the prepared pan.

- Bake the cake until the top springs back when touched in the center, 15 to 18 minutes. Remove from the oven and place the marshmallows evenly over the top of the cake. Return the cake to the oven and continue baking until the marshmallows are soft, 2 to 3 minutes. Gently spread the marshmallows over the cake and immediately spread the frosting over the marshmallow layer. Cool completely before cutting the cake into squares.

[SEE PHOTO ON PAGE 192]

BEIGNETS

Makes about 3 dozen

Pronounced "ben-YAY," these rectangular, no-hole doughnuts are served twenty-four hours a day, seven days a week at Café du Monde in New Orleans. With this recipe you can do them at home. Even at home, they must be served heartily dusted with confectioners' sugar and with a piping hot café au lait made with strong chicory coffee.

These tasty fritters may be served as breakfast, brunch, or dessert.

1	gallon peanut oil for frying
3½	cups sifted, all-purpose flour, plus more for rolling
1	teaspoon baking powder
½	teaspoon salt
4	large eggs, lightly beaten
1	cup sugar
⅓	cup canola oil
⅓	cup milk
¾	cup confectioners' sugar

- Heat the peanut oil in a large, heavy-bottom pot over medium-high heat until the temperature reaches 360°F.
- Sift together the flour, baking powder, and salt in a medium bowl.
- In a large bowl whisk together the eggs and sugar. Add the canola oil and milk. Add the flour mixture to the egg mixture, stirring just until the dough comes together.
- Turn the dough out onto a clean, lightly floured work surface. With a lightly floured rolling pin, roll the dough out to about ⅛ inch thick. Using a sharp knife, pastry wheel, or dough scraper, cut into 2-inch squares.
- Fry until puffy and golden brown on both sides, turning once with tongs. Cooking time is about 3 minutes per side. Remove with a slotted spoon and drain on paper towels. Sift the confectioners' sugar over the hot beignets and serve immediately.

BROILED ORANGES

Makes 4 servings

Navel oranges are seedless and considered to be the best orange to eat out of hand. They have a meaty flesh, they are easy to peel, and the segments separate easily. All navel oranges have a rounded navel at the blossom end, a rounded opening with a dimpled interior that looks, well, like a navel.

Juice oranges are best for juicing. They normally have seeds and thinner rinds. Navel oranges are best for this recipe. If you want a substitute for the sherry, try apple or grape juice.

2	medium navel oranges
1	tablespoon firmly packed brown sugar
1	tablespoon dry sherry
1	tablespoon unsalted butter
	Ground cinnamon
	Ground ginger

- Place the oven rack 6 inches from the heat source. Heat the oven to broil.
- Slice off just the tip of each end of the oranges. Cut each orange in half crosswise. Using a grapefruit or paring knife, carefully cut around segments to separate them from the peel and membrane. Place the orange halves in a small baking dish.
- Divide the brown sugar and sherry among the oranges, sprinkling the tops of each half. Dot each half with butter. Sprinkle each half with the cinnamon and ginger to taste.
- Transfer to the oven and broil until hot and bubbly, about 3 minutes. Serve warm.

Marvin with author and restaurateur Robert St. John
collaborating on a Taste of the South.

HOMEMADE CHOCOLATE PUDDING

Makes 6 servings

Chocolate pudding makes everyone feel like a kid. If you want the pudding slightly more bitter, simply substitute bittersweet for the semisweet chips.

The taste of the chocolate really stands out with the addition of the vanilla extract. Make sure to use pure vanilla extract only, not imitation. To make your own vanilla at home, split six vanilla beans in half lengthwise to reveal their seeds. Put the beans in a quart of best-quality vodka to steep in a dark place at room temperature for one month. After steeping, you'll have a flavorful extract.

¾	cup sugar
⅓	cup cocoa powder
3	tablespoons cornstarch
¼	teaspoon fine salt
2	cups cream
3	ounces semisweet chocolate chips
1	teaspoon pure vanilla extract

- In a medium saucepan whisk together the sugar, cocoa, cornstarch, and salt. Gradually whisk in half the cream until smooth and then whisk in the remaining cream. Set the pan over medium heat and cook, whisking constantly, until the mixture thickens and comes to a boil, about 5 minutes. Continue to whisk and boil for 1 minute.

- Remove the pan from the heat and add the chocolate and vanilla. Let stand for 5 minutes until the chocolate is melted and then stir gently until the pudding is smooth.

- Divide the pudding among six small dessert dishes or pudding cups. Let cool for about 20 minutes to serve warm and soft, or chill for at least 30 minutes or up to 8 hours.

PECAN SANDIES

Makes about 4 dozen cookies

The best way to measure dry ingredients for baking is to use a scale. However, many home cooks do not have a scale and most recipes for home cooks do not list the weight of the ingredients. It's then best to measure the dry ingredients, then sift.

To measure dry ingredients, dip the measuring cup into the flour, fill it, and level the cup off with the back of a knife or a metal spatula. Then sift the flour through a sifter or fine-mesh sieve, and that will remove any lumps. The results will be accurate and correct.

1	cup (2 sticks) unsalted butter, at room temperature
⅓	cup sugar
2½	teaspoons pure vanilla extract
2½	cups all-purpose flour
1	teaspoon salt
1	cup finely chopped pecans
⅓	cup confectioners' sugar for rolling

- Preheat the oven to 350°F. Using the bowl of an electric mixer fitted with a paddle attachment, mix the butter, sugar, and vanilla on medium speed until creamy, about 3 minutes.

- Reduce the speed to low, and add the flour, salt, and pecans, mixing until just blended. Roll into 1-inch balls.

- Bake the balls 1 inch apart on an ungreased baking sheet until lightly browned around the edges, about 15 minutes. Transfer to a wire rack to cool. Roll in confectioners' sugar. Store in airtight container up to two weeks.

APPLE WALNUT CRISP

Makes 8 servings

The trick to making the buttery, nutty topping of a crisp is keeping the butter cold and not overmixing the ingredients. Cut the butter and return it to the refrigerator or freezer while you assemble the rest of the ingredients. Place the dry ingredients in a large, chilled bowl. Cut the butter into the mixture with a pastry cutter until it resembles coarse meal. Using your fingers, gather the mixture into small clumps about the size of peas.

You can also make crumb topping very easily in the bowl of a food processor fitted with the metal blade attachment. First, place the dry mixture in the bowl of the food processor, add the very cold butter, and pulse for about one minute until the mixture resembles coarse meal.

2½	pounds Granny Smith apples, peeled, cored, and sliced ¼ inch thick
2	teaspoons pure vanilla extract
2	tablespoons fresh lemon juice
⅓	cup sugar
1½	tablespoons plus 1 cup all-purpose flour
	Pinch of ground nutmeg
½	cup finely chopped walnuts
¼	cup firmly packed dark brown sugar
½	teaspoon ground cinnamon
	Pinch of salt
½	cup (1 stick) unsalted, chilled butter, cut into ½-inch pieces, plus more for pan
	Whipped cream for serving

- Preheat the oven to 375°F. Butter an 8-inch square glass baking dish. Place the apples, vanilla, and lemon juice in a large bowl and toss to coat. Add the sugar, 1½ tablespoons flour, and nutmeg, stirring to combine.

- Place the remaining 1 cup flour, walnuts, brown sugar, cinnamon, and salt in a medium bowl. Add the butter and cut in, using pastry blender or two knives, until the mixture resembles coarse crumbs. Sprinkle the crumbs over the apples. Bake until golden brown, about 40 minutes. Cool until slightly crisp and serve warm with whipped cream.

PEAR SKILLET CAKE

Makes 8 servings

Bosc pears have a more firm, dense flesh than many other pear varieties, and are perfect for baking, broiling, and poaching. They retain their shape and texture better than other varieties, and their flavor is less likely to be overwhelmed by the use of warm spices like cinnamon, cloves, or nutmeg.

If you have trouble inverting the cake, try heating the bottom of the pan over the burner of the stove to melt and loosen the sugar. If you still have no success, your pan may not be seasoned enough. But no worries—scoop it out and top it with vanilla ice cream. No one will care.

3	firm pears, such as Bosc	1	teaspoon ground ginger
¼	plus ½ cup (1½ sticks total) unsalted butter, room temperature	¼	teaspoon ground cloves
		¼	teaspoon ground nutmeg
1¼	cups firmly packed light brown sugar	½	teaspoon salt
		1	cup unsulfured molasses
2½	cups all-purpose flour	1	cup boiling water
1½	teaspoons baking soda	1	egg, lightly beaten
1	teaspoon ground cinnamon		Vanilla ice cream for serving

- Peel and core the pears and cut into 8 wedges. Melt ¼ cup (½ stick) butter in a cast-iron skillet over medium heat. Reduce the heat to low. Sprinkle ¼ cup brown sugar evenly over the bottom of the skillet and cook, without stirring, 3 minutes (not all the sugar will be melted). Arrange the pears in a circular pattern over the sugar and cook, without stirring, 2 minutes. Remove from the heat.

- Preheat the oven to 350°F. In a medium bowl whisk together flour, baking soda, cinnamon, ginger, cloves, nutmeg, and salt. In a small bowl combine the molasses and boiling water.

- In the bowl of a heavy duty mixer fitted with a paddle attachment on medium speed, combine the remaining ½ cup butter, brown sugar, and egg until creamy, about 2 minutes. Reduce the speed to low and add the flour mixture, alternating with the molasses in three batches until smooth.

- Pour the batter over the pears in the skillet, gently spreading the batter evenly over the pears. Bake until a cake tester inserted into the center of the cake comes out clean, about 45 minutes. Remove to a wire rack to cool 5 minutes.

- Run a thin knife around the edge of the skillet. Place a large serving plate over the skillet. Carefully invert the cake onto the plate. Gently lift off the skillet and replace any pears that remain in the skillet. Serve warm with vanilla ice cream.

ANGEL FOOD CAKE

Makes 10 servings

Cake flour is milled from soft white flour and has lower gluten content than other flour. Gluten is a protein found in wheat flour when liquid is added and mixed. It becomes the framework for any flour mixture and gives cohesiveness to dough. High gluten content is desired when making bread, but low gluten content is desired when making biscuits, cakes, and pastries.

Almost all cake flour is bleached. The bleached flour gives a little acidity to a batter, resulting in a cake with a crumb that's fine and white. Better grocery stores carry cake flour, but it is in a box not a bag as regular flour is. Make sure not to buy self-rising cake flour, which already contains the leavener.

1	cup sifted cake flour
¾	plus ¾ cups sifted sugar
12	large egg whites, room temperature
¼	teaspoon cream of tartar
¼	teaspoon salt
1½	teaspoons pure vanilla extract
1½	teaspoons lemon juice
½	teaspoon almond extract

- Place the rack in the lower third of the oven. Preheat the oven to 325°F. Set aside an ungreased, 10-inch, angel food cake pan.

- In a small bowl combine the flour with ¾ cup sugar. Set the remaining ¾ cup sugar next to the mixer.

- In the bowl of a heavy-duty mixer fitted with the whisk attachment, beat the egg whites at low speed until they begin to froth. Add the cream of tartar and salt, and beat at medium speed until the whites form very soft, billowy mounds. Add the remaining ¾ cup sugar, 1 tablespoon at a time, on medium speed, until all the sugar is added and the whites are shiny and form soft peaks. Add the vanilla, lemon juice, and almond extract and beat until just blended.

- Pour the batter into the ungreased pan and transfer to the oven to bake until golden brown, 50 to 60 minutes. Transfer to a rack to cool, preferably upside-down. Remove from the pan and serve.

KEY LIME PIE

Key limes have a very distinctive aroma and flavor that make them great in the kitchen. They are much smaller than regular Persian limes. No larger than the size of a golf ball, the peel is thin, smooth, and vibrant greenish-yellow when ripe. The flesh is also greenish-yellow, very juicy, and full of seeds.

Instead of substituting for the key limes, try to find the bottled juice at your grocery store, or, better yet, make another dessert and save this delicious recipe for when you can use the real thing.

1¼	cups graham cracker crumbs, about 9 crackers
2	tablespoons sugar
5	tablespoons unsalted butter, melted
1	(14-ounce) can sweetened condensed milk
4	egg yolks
⅔	cup freshly squeezed Key lime juice
	Zest of 2 Key limes
1	cup heavy cream
1	teaspoon pure vanilla extract

- Preheat the oven to 350°F. Mix the graham cracker crumbs, sugar, and butter in a medium bowl with a fork. Press the mixture evenly onto the bottom and sides of a 9-inch glass pie plate. Bake the crust 10 minutes and transfer to a wire rack to cool.

- In a medium bowl whisk together the condensed milk and egg yolks. Add the lime juice and zest, whisking until mixture thickens slightly.

- Pour the filling into the crust and bake 15 minutes. Transfer to a wire rack and cool completely. The filling will set as it cools. Chill to set, covered, in the refrigerator for at least 8 hours.

- Using the bowl of an electric mixer fitted with a whisk attachment, whip the cream and vanilla just until stiff peaks form. Top the pie with the whipped cream and serve.

OLD-SCHOOL HOT FUDGE SAUCE

Makes about 2½ cups

This sauce will firm and harden in the refrigerator. To reheat simply warm it gently over a double boiler. You can purchase a double boiler at a kitchen store, but the simplest solution is to place a heatproof bowl over a saucepan of simmering water.

Make sure to have plenty of this on hand during the summer months when the kids are out of school and ice cream is the most popular dessert.

4	ounces unsweetened chocolate, finely chopped
¼	cup (½ stick) unsalted butter
¼	cup light corn syrup
1½	cups heavy cream
2	cups sugar
2	teaspoons pure vanilla extract
	Pinch of salt

- In a heavy saucepan combine the chocolate, butter, corn syrup, cream, and sugar over low heat. Using a wooden spoon, stir frequently until the chocolate is melted and the sugar is dissolved.

- Increase the heat to medium and bring to a boil without stirring for 8 minutes. Remove from the heat and add the vanilla and a pinch of salt.

- Serve warm over ice cream. Store in an airtight container in the refrigerator for up to one month.

AMBROSIA

To crack a coconut, preheat the oven to 350°F. Pierce three holes on the coconut with an ice pick or a clean screwdriver and drain the juice. Heat the drained coconut in the oven for about 10 minutes to crack the shell. Remove the coconut from the oven and place it in a kitchen towel on the floor or sturdy work surface. Give it a couple of whacks with the hammer to break it completely open. Remove the pieces of broken coconut. The coconut meat will pull easily from the shell. Remove the brown skin from the coconut meat with a vegetable peeler and grate the meat in a food processor or on a box grater.

This simple combination of winter fruit is a southern holiday favorite. Some families add marshmallows or maraschino cherries. Use this as a guide and create your own ambrosia.

6	navel oranges
1	pineapple, peeled, cored, and cut into cubes
1	cup shredded fresh coconut
¼	cup sugar (or to taste)
1	banana
	Mint for garnish

- Peel the oranges, taking care to remove all the white pith. Slice the oranges into ¼-inch circles and place in a large bowl.

- Add the pineapple and coconut to the orange slices and gently toss to combine. Add the sugar to taste. The ambrosia can be refrigerated up to two days, covered.

- When ready to serve, slice the banana and toss it with the other fruits. Garnish with the mint and serve in champagne flutes.

PECAN BROWNIES

Makes 1 (9-inch square) pan

When melting chocolate over a double boiler, it's very important that the chocolate not come into contact with any liquid whatsoever—and that includes steam. Melted chocolate hardens and clumps into a horrible, solid mass when it comes into contact with any liquid, even a drop of water. This is known as "seizing."

If this happens, try adding a tablespoon of vegetable oil to the mixture immediately. Set the hardened chocolate in a pot over simmering water, and try to melt once again. This solution can sometimes save the day, but be prepared to start again.

2	ounces unsweetened chocolate, chopped
1/2	cup semisweet chocolate chips
6	tablespoons (3/4 stick) unsalted butter, plus more for the pan
1 1/3	cups sugar
3	large eggs, lightly beaten
1	teaspoon pure vanilla extract
3/4	cup all-purpose flour, plus more for the pan
1/2	teaspoon salt
3/4	cup coarsely chopped pecans

- Preheat the oven to 350°F. Butter and flour a 9-inch square baking pan, tapping out the excess flour.

- Using a heatproof bowl set over a pan of just simmering water, combine the chocolates and butter. Heat, stirring, until just melted. Remove from the heat and set aside to cool slightly.

- In a large bowl whisk together the sugar, eggs, and vanilla until combined. Whisk in the chocolate mixture. Add the flour and salt. Add the pecans and spread the batter evenly into the prepared pan. Bake in the middle of the oven until a tester inserted into the center comes out with a few crumbs remaining on the tester, about 35 minutes. Transfer to a wire rack to cool. Serve immediately.

UPSIDE-DOWN APPLE CAKE

Makes 1 (10-inch) cake

This cake is deliciously scented and spicy due to the Chinese five-spice powder. Five-spice powder contains cinnamon, cloves, ground star anise, fennel, and Szechwan peppercorns. These peppercorns, which give the powder a very distinctive aroma.

Top this cake with crème frâiche or sour cream for a change of pace. Crème frâiche is commonly used in French cooking. It is a thick, tangy, nutty cream often used in sauces and as a condiment for fresh fruits and desserts. To make it at home, combine 1 cup heavy whipping cream with 2 tablespoons buttermilk in a glass jar. Cover and let it stand at room temperature for 8 to 24 hours, or until thickened.

DROPPIN' KNOWLEDGE

When brown sugar comes into contact with air, the moisture evaporates and causes the sugar to lump together and become hard. Prevent this by storing brown sugar in a sealable plastic bag or in an airtight container. Storing brown sugar in the refrigerator will also help keep it fresh and soft.

FOR THE TOPPING:

3	tablespoons unsalted butter
½	cup firmly packed light brown sugar
1	pound Granny Smith apples, peeled, cored, and cut into thin wedges

FOR THE CAKE:

1	cup all-purpose flour
¼	cup sugar
1	teaspoon baking powder
½	teaspoon baking soda
½	teaspoon salt
1	teaspoon five-spice powder
5	tablespoons unsalted butter, chilled and cut into pieces
½	cup buttermilk
	Crème fraîche or sour cream for serving

- Preheat the oven to 425°F.
- For the topping, using an ovenproof, 10-inch cast-iron skillet over medium heat, heat the butter until the foam subsides. Add the brown sugar and remove from the heat. Spread the mixture evenly in a skillet and arrange the apples, overlapping, in a single layer.
- For the cake, using a food processor fitted with a blade attachment, combine the flour, sugar, baking powder, soda, salt, and five-spice powder. Add the butter and pulse just until the mixture resembles coarse meal. Transfer to a medium bowl and add the buttermilk, stirring until just moistened.
- Drop the batter by spoonfuls on top of the apples and gently spread the batter, leaving a 1-inch border around the edge of the skillet to allow room for the cake to expand.
- Bake the cake until golden brown and firm to the touch, about 25 minutes. Transfer to a wire rack and cool for 3 minutes. Carefully invert onto a serving platter. Replace any apples that stick to the skillet on the cake. Serve warm with crème fraîche or sour cream, if desired.

MERINGUE KISSES

Makes about 2 dozen

Simply put, meringue is egg whites that have been beaten with sugar to form a thick, stiff foam. Different textures are achieved by varying the methods of mixing the sugar and the egg whites, and by varying the baking times and temperatures. Meringue can top a lemon meringue pie, cover a retro baked Alaska, or be dried in the oven as a Pavlova or meringue cookie.

One way or the other, you can't beat a meringue for a fat-free dessert. The fat from whole eggs is located in the yolk. The whites are fat free.

2	egg whites
½	cup sugar

- Preheat the oven to 200°F. Line a baking sheet with parchment paper.
- Using the bowl of an electric mixer fitted with a whisk attachment, whisk the egg whites on medium speed until soft peaks form. Increase the speed to medium high. Gradually add the sugar, whisking until stiff, glossy peaks form. Drop heaping teaspoons (not measuring spoons) of meringue onto the prepared baking sheet about 1 inch apart.
- Bake on the center rack of the oven until crisp and dry, about 45 minutes. Turn the oven off and leave the meringues in the oven at least 1 hour and preferably overnight.
- Using a metal spatula, transfer the meringues to a rack to cool completely. Store in an airtight container at room temperature two to three days.

BANANAS FOSTER

Makes 2 servings

Bananas Foster rivals beignets for being the most popular sweet in the city of New Orleans. It's traditionally made at Brennan's Restaurant with rum, brown sugar, and banana liqueur and served over vanilla ice cream. In this recipe, toasted pecans and cinnamon give it a little kick.

This is a great last-minute dessert for an every-night supper—and a great way to use up on-the-way-out bananas.

1	tablespoon unsalted butter
2	ripe bananas, peeled and cut horizontally (the riper the better)
2	tablespoons firmly packed brown sugar
½	cup pecans, toasted
¼	teaspoon ground cinnamon
½	teaspoon pure vanilla extract
2	tablespoons dark rum
	Vanilla ice cream for serving

- Using a medium sauté pan over medium heat, melt the butter and sauté the halved bananas for 1 minute. Add the sugar and pecans, stirring gently to melt and combine, about 1 minute. Add the cinnamon, vanilla, and rum. Stir to combine and serve immediately over vanilla ice cream.

TAPIOCA PUDDING

Makes 4 servings

Tapioca pudding is one of those down-home desserts; it's soft and creamy comfort food. The best part is that it takes very little time to put together.

If you don't have maple syrup, simply substitute two tablespoons brown sugar. And, for the vanilla bean, use one teaspoon pure vanilla extract. It won't be as attractive visually, but it will taste great.

2	cups whole milk
1/4	cup sugar
3	tablespoons quick-cooking tapioca
2	tablespoons pure maple syrup
1	large egg
1/4	teaspoon salt
1	cinnamon stick
1	whole vanilla bean, split lengthwise, seeds scraped and saved

- Using a medium saucepan, combine the milk, sugar, tapioca, syrup, egg, salt, cinnamon stick, vanilla bean, and seeds. Whisk to combine. Let stand, without stirring, 5 minutes. Place over medium heat and cook, stirring constantly, until the mixture comes to a boil. Remove the cinnamon stick and vanilla bean.

- Divide among four individual serving cups and cover with plastic wrap. Refrigerate until cool, stirring occasionally, about 20 minutes. The pudding may be stored, covered, in the refrigerator up to one day.

DROPPIN' KNOWLEDGE

When working with a vanilla bean allow the bean to steep in the liquid. Remove the bean and split it down the center. Take the back of your knife and press against the bean to get all of the seeds out and add that to your liquid, as well.

SPICED FRUIT COMPOTE

Makes 6 servings

Compotes have a long culinary history. They are fresh or dried fruit cooked in syrup, usually with spices and citrus zest, and served as a dessert. It's a nice dessert for the winter when fewer fruits are in season, and it has that old-fashioned quality of using what was "put up" in the summer.

Other herbs and spices to try are fresh bay leaves, thyme, lemon zest, and a cinnamon stick.

1	sprig fresh rosemary, leaves only
2	(5-inch-long) strips orange zest
1	teaspoon whole black peppercorns
3	cups freshly squeezed orange juice
2	cups dried peaches
¾	cup dried tart cherries
¾	cup raisins
¾	cup dry white wine
¾	cup sugar
	Frozen yogurt for serving

- Place the rosemary, orange zest, and peppercorns on a large square of three layers of moistened cheesecloth. Gather the cheesecloth and tie securely.

- Place the cheesecloth bundle along with the orange juice, dried peaches, cherries, raisins, white wine, and sugar in a large saucepan. Bring to a boil over high heat, stirring until the sugar dissolves. Reduce the heat to medium low, and simmer, uncovered, until the fruit is tender and the liquid is thick and syrupy, stirring occasionally, about 35 minutes.

- Transfer the compote with the cheesecloth bundle to a large bowl; chill until cold, at least 6 hours. Using tongs, remove the cheesecloth bundle. Serve the compote with frozen yogurt or ice cream.

CARROT CAKE

Makes 1 (9-inch square) cake

Carrot Cake is moist, spicy, and sweet and coated in a tangy, sweet cream cheese frosting. The oil is what makes the cake so moist and it's a southern staple on the dessert buffet. Make sure to use canola, vegetable, or corn oil—a light, flavorless oil that won't overpower the spices.

This frosting is extra rich and creamy with the addition of the white chocolate. To add texture, coat the frosted cake in chopped, toasted pecans.

1½	cups all-purpose flour, plus more for the pan	½	cup grated carrot	
½	cup granulated sugar	½	cup canned crushed pineapple with juice	
½	cup firmly packed light brown sugar	½	cup golden raisins	
1	teaspoon baking powder	¼	cup freshly grated coconut or unsweetened flaked coconut	
1	teaspoon baking soda	2	teaspoons pure vanilla extract	
1	teaspoon ground cinnamon	1	recipe Cream Cheese Frosting (page 218), or confectioners' sugar for dusting (optional)	
½	teaspoon ground nutmeg			
½	teaspoon salt			
2	large eggs, room temperature			
⅔	cup canola oil			

- Preheat the oven to 350°F. Coat a 9-inch square baking pan with vegetable cooking spray and dust it with flour.

- In a medium bowl stir together the flour, sugars, baking powder, baking soda, cinnamon, nutmeg, and salt.

- In a large bowl whisk together the eggs and oil. Add the egg mixture to the dry ingredients and stir until just combined. Add the carrot, pineapple, raisins, coconut, and vanilla. Stir until just combined. Transfer the batter to the prepared pan.

- Bake for 35 to 40 minutes, or until a toothpick inserted into the center of the cake comes out clean. Remove to a wire rack and let it cool for 15 minutes. Remove the cake from the pan, and frost it with Cream Cheese Frosting or dust it with confectioners' sugar, if desired.

CREAM CHEESE FROSTING

Makes frosting for 1 (9-inch, 2-layer) cake

8 ounces cream cheese, softened

¼ cup (½ stick) unsalted butter, room temperature

1 teaspoon pure vanilla extract

3 cups confectioners' sugar, sifted

3 ounces white chocolate, melted then cooled

- In the bowl of a heavy-duty mixer fitted with the paddle attachment, cream together the cream cheese, butter, and vanilla until combined.

- Gradually add the confectioners' sugar until combined. Beat in the white chocolate. (If the frosting seems to be a little thick, thin it with a touch of milk.) This will keep for one week in a covered container in the refrigerator.

INDEX

Page numbers in italics refer to photographs